AF480912

# VERBATIQUE

*The Power of Communication*

***By***

Mr. Dimpu Sarath Kumar

Mr. Sai Gupta

Mrs. Venkata Ravali

Mrs. Sridevi Kanulla

**Title**: *Verbatique*

**Contributors**: *Dimpu Sarath Kumar, Sai Gupta, Venkata Ravali, Sridevi Kanulla*

**Owned by: Intact Intern Stump Solutions Private Limited**

**Disclaimer**:

*VERBATIQUE: The Power of Communication is for educational purposes only. The author and publisher are not responsible for any outcomes resulting from the application of the concepts presented. While every effort has been made to ensure accuracy, communication is context-dependent, and results may vary. Readers are encouraged to seek professional advice when necessary. The content reflects the author's personal views and experiences.*

**First Edition: 2025**

## AUTHORS' BIOGRAPHY:

***Mr. Dimpu Sarath Kumar:*** *Dimpu Sarath Kumar is an Entrepreneur. He is the Founder and CEO of Intern Stump. Despite coming from a middle-class background, he began his entrepreneurial journey at 22 to provide skill-based training to rural and semi-urban students. His leadership blends technology, education, and impact-driven solutions to shape a future-ready generation.*

## CO-AUTHORS' BIOGRAPHY:

***Mr. Sai Gupta:*** *Sai Gupta, a visionary entrepreneur and Co-Founder of Intern Stump, was born and raised in a small town with big dreams. From an early age, he exhibited a keen interest in numbers and finance, foreshadowing the remarkable journey that awaited him in the world of business. Sai is committed to empowering learners and building sustainable growth in the education sector.*

***Mrs. Venkata Ravali:*** *Mrs. Venkata Ravali is a dynamic expert in Human Resource Management, Professional Communication, and Product Management. She empowers individuals and organizations through strategic HR practices and impactful communication training. Her work in product management bridges innovation with client-centric solutions.*

***Mrs. Sridevi Kanulla:*** *Mrs. Sridevi Kanulla is a passionate educator and communication mentor dedicated to empowering expressive individuals. As a co-author, she contributed select insights to Verbatique, enriching it with her unique perspective on effective communication. Her work continues to inspire learners to embrace clarity and confidence in their interactions.*

# TABLE OF CONTENTS


| Title of the Content | Page |
|---|---|
| Introduction To the Verbatique | *6-11* *(Index)* |
| Chapter – I : Core Concepts and Cultural Roots | *1-37* |
| Chapter – II : The Workplace Lens | *38-61* |
| Chapter – III : Global and Cross-Cultural Communication | *62-81* |
| Chapter – IV : Communication for Growth and Success | *82-103* |
| Chapter – V : The Power of Speaking, Listening, Reading and Writing | *104-155* |
| The Power of Communication in Shaping Our World | *156-157* |

# PREFACE

Communication is at the heart of everything we do, shaping our interactions, relationships, and the way we navigate the world. Whether in personal conversations, professional settings, or cross-cultural exchanges, the ability to connect meaningfully through words is more important than ever. *VERBATIQUE: The Power of Communication* is a journey into the core principles of effective communication.

This book is rooted in the understanding that communication is a dynamic, evolving process that requires both skill and mindfulness. It explores not just the art of speaking, but also the essential role of listening, understanding diverse perspectives, and adapting to various situations. From overcoming misunderstandings and conflicts to mastering professional communication.

The ideas within these pages are drawn from years of research, observation, and real-world experience. Ultimately, the goal of *VERBATIQUE* is to inspire a shift in how we approach communication. In a world that is increasingly diverse and interconnected, our words have the power to build, to bridge gaps, and to create lasting change. As you explore the concepts and techniques in this book, we hope you'll find new ways to communicate with purpose, clarity, and empathy, and discover the transformative potential of every conversation you have.

*With sincerity and purpose,*

***Authors***

# ACKNOWLEDGMENT

*We would like to express our sincere gratitude to all those who have supported us throughout the creation of VERBATIQUE: The Power of Communication. This book would not have been possible without the encouragement, insight, and feedback from numerous individuals who have shared their wisdom and experiences.*

*First and foremost, we extend our heartfelt thanks to our families for their unwavering love, patience, and understanding as we dedicated countless hours to bring this project to life.*

*We are deeply grateful to our mentors, colleagues, and friends who offered their guidance, expertise, and constructive criticism. Your perspectives on communication, whether from the workplace or beyond, have enriched this book and made it more relevant to a diverse audience.*

*Special thanks to the readers who have continuously inspired us with their desire to grow and enhance their communication skills. Your curiosity and willingness to learn have driven us to explore new approaches and present them in a way that is both accessible and practical.*

*Lastly, we would like to acknowledge the Intern Stump team behind the production of VERBATIQUE, from the editors to the designers and everyone involved in bringing this book into being. Your dedication and attention to detail have played a crucial role in ensuring the quality and clarity of this work.*

*We hope this book will inspire you to improve the way you communicate, build stronger relationships, and contribute to creating a world where words have the power to build, not break.*

***With gratitude,***

***Dimpu Sarath Kumar, Sai Gupta, Venkata Ravali, Sridevi Kanulla***

## INTRODUCTION TO VERBATIQUE

*The Power of Communication*

Communication is one of the most vital life skills that influences every aspect of human interaction. From our earliest moments to our most complex endeavors, we rely on our ability to express, listen, understand, and connect. Communication is more than just exchanging words. It is a bridge between people, a tool for building relationships, a medium for expressing identity, and a means for creating progress.

In the modern world, communication has evolved beyond face-to-face conversations. We now communicate across digital platforms, in professional settings, in multicultural environments, and through various mediums that did not exist a few decades ago. Despite this evolution, the core principles of communication remain unchanged. What has changed is the urgency and complexity of how we apply these principles in our daily lives.

This book, *VERBATIQUE: The Power of Communication*, is designed to explore and deepen your understanding of communication from all angles. It is written with a strong purpose in mind: to help you become a more confident, thoughtful, and effective communicator. Whether you are a student, a professional, an educator, a leader, or someone looking to strengthen personal connections, this book aims to serve as your companion on the journey of communication mastery.

The chapters that follow reflect a practical and realistic view of communication. Rather than simply offering definitions and techniques, the content is grounded in real-life relevance. It considers the daily challenges people face in expressing themselves, listening actively, managing workplace conversations, overcoming cultural gaps, and building meaningful human connections. Each chapter is a step forward in understanding not only what communication is but what it can become when approached with intention.

In today's fast-paced society, where attention spans are shrinking and digital noise is rising, authentic communication is becoming rare. We often mistake talking for communicating and assume that information shared is information understood. This book challenges that assumption. It offers a deep dive into various aspects of communication to show that true effectiveness comes from clarity, empathy, consistency, and awareness.

The purpose of communication goes beyond just sharing facts or persuading someone. At its best, communication helps people feel heard, seen, and valued. It creates environments where ideas are respected, feedback is welcomed, and diversity is embraced. A strong communicator not only conveys a message but also considers the impact it creates on the listener. This book teaches you how to be conscious of that impact and how to improve the quality of your interactions.

One of the central themes of this book is the idea of human-centric communication. In our interactions, we often focus on content, tone, timing, and presentation. While these are all important, they should be guided by empathy. Empathy allows us to understand where the other person is coming from, and how they might interpret our message. When we lead with empathy, we speak in ways that connect rather than divide, clarify rather than confuse, and empower rather than intimidate.

Another theme this book explores is the importance of communication in leadership. Leaders are often judged not only by their decisions but by how they communicate them. A good leader inspires confidence, motivates action, and fosters collaboration through words and presence. Leadership communication is not just about authority or confidence.

It is about being approachable, honest, and respectful. This book provides practical ways to develop leadership presence through effective communication strategies.

Similarly, communication in academic and professional settings comes with its own expectations. Students today must be able to express their ideas clearly in writing, speak effectively during interviews, and participate in group discussions with confidence. Professionals are expected to communicate with clients, colleagues, and superiors in a manner that reflects both professionalism and competence. This book addresses these needs through structured chapters that break down the components of speaking, writing, reading, and listening.

Clarity is another pillar of this book. Many communication problems stem from unclear messages. Whether it is in writing or speech, clarity improves understanding, saves time, and prevents confusion. To achieve clarity, one must be mindful of the language used, the structure of the message, and the medium of delivery. This book walks you through techniques to simplify complex ideas, organize your thoughts, and ensure that your message reaches the intended audience with minimal distortion.

The book also tackles misunderstandings and conflicts. Every person brings their own experiences, assumptions, and emotions to a conversation. These differences can create friction. But with the right mindset and approach, communication can be a way to resolve conflicts rather than escalate them. The book provides tools to listen actively, respond respectfully, and manage tense situations with professionalism.

Cross-cultural communication is another key area explored in this book. In an increasingly globalized world, we often find ourselves interacting with people from different cultural backgrounds. What is considered polite in one culture may seem rude in another. These cultural differences, if not acknowledged, can lead to miscommunication. The book encourages readers to adopt a mindset of cultural humility and offers guidance on how to adapt communication styles to diverse environments.

For students and learners, communication skills are not just soft skills. They are essential for academic success, career advancement, and personal development. A student who can articulate thoughts clearly, ask relevant questions, and present ideas convincingly gains a major advantage in both the classroom and the job market. This book includes dedicated sections to help learners master the communication skills that will serve them throughout life.

The workplace is another setting where communication can make or break careers. From writing emails to giving presentations, from participating in meetings to leading teams, professionals are constantly judged by how they communicate. This book equips you with the practical knowledge and mindset to handle workplace communication with confidence and effectiveness. It teaches you how to listen to feedback, how to manage up and down the hierarchy, and how to communicate under pressure.

In job interviews and resume writing, communication plays a critical role. A well-written resume and a confident interview presence can open doors. This book shows how to present your strengths, experiences, and value in ways that resonate with recruiters and employers. It emphasizes authenticity and preparation as the foundations of impactful communication in career settings.

In addition to professional and academic communication, this book highlights the emotional and relational side of how we communicate. The words we use with family, friends, and even strangers shape the quality of our relationships. By communicating with kindness, clarity, and patience, we create a space where trust can grow and conflicts can be resolved. The book encourages readers to reflect on their daily conversations and become more aware of their communication patterns.

Communication is not just about talking. It is equally about listening. Listening is a skill that many overlook but is central to meaningful interactions. Listening helps us understand others better, respond more thoughtfully, and avoid unnecessary mistakes. This book places a strong emphasis on developing active listening habits that enhance both personal and professional relationships.

Reading and writing are also powerful forms of communication that often determine how people perceive our intelligence, credibility, and attention to detail. Being able to read efficiently and write clearly can save time, reduce errors, and increase productivity. This book provides techniques for reading with purpose, comprehending better, and writing with structure and style.

At the core of all communication is the intent to connect. Whether we are trying to inform, persuade, entertain, or comfort, our words carry the power to influence how others feel and act. This book helps readers become more conscious of that power and how to use it responsibly. Through practical examples, reflective exercises, and real-world scenarios, readers will gain a toolkit for becoming more persuasive, more thoughtful, and more impactful communicators.

Communication is also shaped by the context in which it happens. The same message may be received differently depending on the environment, the timing, and the relationship between the people involved. This book emphasizes the importance of being sensitive to these variables. It encourages readers to pause, assess the situation, and then choose the most appropriate communication approach.

As you read through this book, you will discover that communication is a skill that can be learned, practiced, and improved. It is not something we are born knowing. It is a lifelong learning process that evolves with our experiences. The book encourages readers to be open to feedback, to reflect on their communication patterns, and to commit to continuous improvement.

Ultimately, *VERBATIQUE: The Power of Communication* is about empowerment. It is about helping people find their voice, build meaningful relationships, and create positive change through communication. It is a reminder that our words matter and that we have the ability to shape the world around us through how we choose to speak, write, read, and listen.

This book is a call to action. It invites readers to move beyond passive communication and become intentional communicators. It challenges assumptions, offers practical advice, and promotes empathy and clarity in every interaction. Whether you are at the start of your communication journey or looking to refine your existing skills, this book is here to guide you.

As we begin this journey together, remember that communication is not about perfection. It is about connection. It is about understanding and being understood. It is about creating space for dialogue, growth, and shared meaning. With this in mind, let us begin our exploration of the power of communication. Let us learn, practice, reflect, and improve. Let us choose words that build, uplift, and inspire.

Welcome to *VERBATIQUE*.

# CHAPTER - I : CORE CONCEPTS AND CULTURAL ROOTS

*Understanding Foundations of Human Communication*

## *Part-1: The Power of Communication: The Foundation of All Human Interaction*

Communication is the backbone of human existence. It is the very essence that shapes our relationships, drives our societies, and enables progress. From the first utterances of a newborn to the complex discourse of political leaders, communication transcends boundaries, allowing us to connect, understand, and collaborate. As humans, our ability to communicate is what differentiates us from other species and is at the core of all human interaction. This exploration into the power of communication uncovers its fundamental role in shaping our world.

**The Significance of Communication in Human Life**: At its core, communication is the process of transmitting information from one person to another. It is not just about the words we speak but also the body language, tone, and context in which we engage.

Whether verbal or non-verbal, communication allows individuals to express their thoughts, share feelings, and influence others. Without it, societies would fall into isolation, progress would stagnate, and individuals would be unable to form meaningful relationships.

In the simplest terms, communication is an essential tool for survival and thriving. It allows us to convey ideas, solve problems, and work together. Without effective communication, misunderstandings can arise, relationships can deteriorate, and societies can crumble. Thus, communication is not merely a tool but a vital pillar upon which the foundation of human society is built.

**Evolution of Communication**: Human communication has evolved dramatically over the millennia. Initially, early humans communicated through gestures and vocal sounds, which gradually developed into more structured forms of speech. This primitive form of communication laid the groundwork for the complex systems we use today. Over time, languages were born, and societies began to develop written forms of communication, further enhancing our ability to share knowledge across generations.

The invention of the printing press in the 15th century marked another turning point in the evolution of communication. It allowed information to be disseminated more widely and quickly, democratizing knowledge. In the 20th century, the advent of electronic media, including radio, television, and the internet, revolutionized how people communicated. Today, technology continues to shape communication, with social media platforms, instant messaging, and video calls becoming integral parts of daily life.

This historical journey shows that communication has always been essential for human development. From the early days of primitive gestures to the digital era, it has continuously evolved to meet the needs of individuals and societies.

**Types of Communication**: Communication can be categorized into several different types, each serving a specific purpose in human interaction. The most commonly recognized types of communication are verbal, non-verbal, and written.

**(i) Verbal Communication**: Verbal communication is the use of words to convey messages. It can be spoken or written, with speech being the most direct and immediate form. Verbal communication allows for clarity and precision, as individuals can express their thoughts, ideas, and emotions in real-time. However, it also requires a shared understanding of language and context for effective transmission. Miscommunication often arises when the speaker and the listener do not share the same frame of reference.

Verbal communication can take place in various forms, such as face-to-face conversations, telephone calls, video conferences, and public speeches. The richness of verbal communication lies in its ability to convey detailed information, elicit emotional responses, and foster understanding.

**(ii) Non-Verbal Communication**: Non-verbal communication is perhaps the most powerful and subtle form of communication. It includes body language, facial expressions, eye contact, gestures, and posture. Unlike verbal communication, non-verbal cues often convey more about a person's emotions and intentions than words alone. In fact, studies have shown that a significant portion of our communication is non-verbal. This is because body language can reveal our true feelings, even when our words suggest otherwise.

Non-verbal communication also plays a crucial role in reinforcing or contradicting verbal messages. For instance, if a person says they are fine but their body language suggests otherwise, the listener will likely sense something is amiss. Thus, non-verbal communication is a powerful tool in fostering trust and understanding.

**(iii) Written Communication**: Written communication involves the use of written symbols to convey information. This can range from formal documents like emails and letters to informal text messages. Written communication allows for more thoughtful and deliberate expression, as it gives the writer time to organize their thoughts and present them clearly.

In the digital age, written communication has expanded to include emails, blogs, social media posts, and text messages, making it easier to communicate across distances. While it lacks the immediacy of verbal communication, written communication offers the advantage of permanence and the ability to reference messages later.

**The Role of Communication in Building Relationships**: Human relationships are built on the foundation of communication. From the earliest stages of life, communication enables individuals to connect, share experiences, and understand each other. Whether in families, friendships, romantic partnerships, or professional environments, effective communication is essential for building trust, resolving conflicts, and deepening bonds.

In relationships, communication is not just about speaking or writing; it is also about listening. Active listening is a crucial component of communication, as it allows individuals to understand the thoughts, emotions, and perspectives of others. When both parties engage in active listening, they create an environment of mutual respect and understanding.

**Communication in the Workplace**: In the professional world, communication is integral to the success of teams, organizations, and businesses. Effective communication within the workplace can increase productivity, foster collaboration, and improve employee morale. Clear communication is essential for conveying expectations, delegating tasks, and ensuring that everyone is on the same page.

In today's globalized world, businesses often communicate across different cultures and languages. This has created a need for cross-cultural communication skills, as misunderstandings can arise when individuals from different backgrounds interact. By learning to recognize and respect cultural differences, businesses can build more inclusive and effective communication strategies.

**The Impact of Technology on Communication**: Technology has transformed the way we communicate. The rise of social media, instant messaging, and video conferencing has made it easier to stay connected with others, regardless of geographical distance. Technology has also opened up new avenues for communication, allowing people to communicate more quickly and efficiently.

However, the shift to digital communication has also brought challenges. Online communication often lacks the richness of face-to-face interaction, and the nuances of non-verbal communication are often lost. Furthermore, the overreliance on digital communication can lead to misunderstandings, as tone and intent are sometimes difficult to discern in written messages.

Despite these challenges, technology has revolutionized the way we connect with others, enabling us to communicate in real-time, collaborate on projects, and share information instantly.

**Barriers to Effective Communication**: Despite its power, communication is not always effective. Several barriers can hinder the transmission of messages, leading to misunderstandings and conflicts. These barriers include language differences, cultural misunderstandings, emotional biases, physical distractions, and technological issues.

Language differences can create significant challenges, especially in a multicultural or international context. Misunderstandings can arise when individuals speak different languages or use words with different meanings. Similarly, cultural differences can affect communication styles, as different cultures have varying norms and expectations regarding communication.

Emotional biases can also distort communication. For instance, when individuals are angry, frustrated, or anxious, they may struggle to communicate clearly and may misinterpret the intentions of others. Physical distractions, such as noise or poor internet connections, can also disrupt communication and prevent effective message transmission.

**Improving Communication Skills**: Given the importance of communication in all aspects of life, improve our communication skills is essential. Effective communicators are not only able to express their thoughts and ideas clearly but also understand the perspectives of others. Developing strong communication skills requires practice, self-awareness, and the willingness to adapt.

One of the most important aspects of communication is active listening. By focusing on what others are saying, asking clarifying questions, and responding thoughtfully, we can improve our understanding of their needs and concerns. Additionally, being aware of our non-verbal cues, such as body language and facial expressions, can help us communicate more effectively. Furthermore, improving our written communication skills can help us present ideas in a clear and structured manner. By paying attention to grammar, tone, and the clarity of our writing, we can ensure that our messages are well-received.

**The Future of Communication**: As society continues to evolve, so too will the ways in which we communicate. With advancements in artificial intelligence, virtual reality, and augmented reality, communication is set to become even more immersive and interactive. New technologies will likely enhance our ability to connect with others, breaking down geographical barriers and enabling more dynamic and real-time communication.

However, with these advances, it will be crucial to continue emphasizing the importance of human connection. While technology can enhance communication, it should never replace the fundamental human need for personal interaction.

Communication is the foundation of all human interaction. It is the tool through which we express ourselves, build relationships, and advance societies. From its early roots in gestures and vocal sounds to its present-day forms of digital communication, the evolution of communication has been pivotal in shaping the human experience. As technology continues to transform the way we connect, communication remains as crucial as ever in ensuring that we understand one another, resolve conflicts, and work together to build a better future. By honing our communication skills, we can navigate the complexities of the modern world and strengthen the bonds that tie us all together.

***Section Closed...***

## *Part-2: The Origins of Human Communication: Evolution Across Early Civilizations*

Communication is one of the most powerful tools ever developed by human beings. It is not just the act of speaking or writing but the exchange of ideas, emotions, and information. Without communication, human societies would not have advanced to the level we see today. It connects people across regions, cultures, and generations. When we hear the word "communication," we may think of modern tools like mobile phones, the internet, or even printed books. But the origin of communication goes far back into ancient times. It is as old as human existence itself.

Understanding the history of communication helps us appreciate the journey from the simplest methods to the complex technologies of today. The development of communication mirrors the evolution of human civilization. From primitive drawings on cave walls to digital communication, the methods have changed drastically, but the purpose has remained the same: to connect, to express, and to share.

**The Earliest Forms of Communication:** The earliest human beings communicated without spoken language. Before language evolved, humans used hand gestures, facial expressions, body posture, and even eye contact. These were non-verbal forms of communication that played a crucial role in survival and social bonding.

Soon after, humans began to use sounds to express emotions. Grunts, cries, and laughter helped to build early forms of interaction. These sounds later developed into more structured systems that led to spoken languages.

**Cave Paintings and Symbolic Communication:** As human intelligence grew, so did the need to express more complex ideas. This led to the creation of symbolic communication. Around 30,000 years ago, humans began drawing on cave walls. These drawings were not just art but also a way to tell stories, record events, or communicate beliefs.

The Lascaux Caves in France are famous for their ancient paintings. These paintings included images of animals, human figures, and symbolic signs. They reflect the early human desire to communicate ideas and experiences visually. This was one of the earliest steps toward written communication.

**The Birth of Language:** The exact time and place where spoken language first appeared is unknown. However, most scholars agree that language developed over thousands of years. As humans began living in larger groups, they needed better ways to coordinate, share information, and pass down knowledge. Language allowed this to happen.

Languages likely started with simple words and sounds and became more complex over generations. With time, different groups of people developed their own languages, leading to the diverse linguistic landscape we see today.

**The Invention of Writing:** The invention of writing marks a major turning point in the history of communication. Writing allowed humans to record ideas and pass them on to others across time and distance. This was essential for the development of societies, trade, religion, and governance.

The earliest known writing systems appeared around 3000 BCE. In Mesopotamia, the Sumerians developed a system called cuneiform. They used a reed stylus to press wedge-shaped marks into clay tablets. Around the same time, in Egypt, hieroglyphics were developed. These were more pictorial and decorative but served similar purposes in recording information. Writing made it possible to create records, laws, religious texts, and literature. It brought structure and permanence to communication.

**The Role of the Alphabet:** As writing evolved, it became more efficient. Around 1200 BCE, the Phoenicians created the first known alphabet. It was a system of symbols that represented sounds. This was a significant advancement because it made writing easier to learn and use.

The Phoenician alphabet influenced other cultures, including the Greeks, who adapted it and added vowels. The Greek alphabet then became the basis for the Latin alphabet, which is used in many modern languages, including English. Alphabets simplified communication and opened the door for wider literacy. People could now learn to read and write more easily, and ideas could spread more quickly.

**Oral Traditions and Storytelling:** Even with the rise of writing, oral traditions remained strong for many centuries. In many cultures, history, religion, and values were passed down through spoken stories. Storytelling was not just entertainment. It was a way of preserving knowledge, identity, and wisdom.

Epic poems like the "Iliad" and the "Odyssey" were passed down orally before being written. In India, the Vedas were memorized and recited for generations. African tribes used storytelling to keep their histories alive. These traditions show how communication was both a personal and a community activity.

**Communication in the Ancient World:** Ancient civilizations developed various systems for long-distance communication. The Persians built a system of roads and relay stations for delivering messages quickly. The Romans used signal towers and runners to send information across their empire.

Paper was invented in China around 100 BCE, which led to the development of printing. With paper, writing became easier and more widespread. The Chinese also used smoke signals and drums for military communication. These early systems show how societies valued communication and invested in improving it.

**The Printing Revolution:** One of the most important events in the history of communication was the invention of the printing press. In the mid-1400s, Johannes Gutenberg developed a printing press that used movable type. This allowed books to be printed in large numbers, quickly and affordably.

Before this, books were copied by hand, which was slow and expensive. The printing press made books available to more people, leading to a rise in literacy and education. It also allowed for the spread of new ideas, such as those from the Renaissance and the Reformation.

The printing press marked the beginning of mass communication. For the first time, information could reach thousands of people at once.

**Newspapers and Periodicals:** As printing technology improved, newspapers and magazines became popular. The first regular newspapers appeared in the 1600s in

Europe. These publications provided news, opinions, and information about trade and politics.

Newspapers helped to shape public opinion and informed people about local and global events. They became a powerful tool for communication and social change.

By the 1800s, daily newspapers were common in major cities. The rise of journalism created a new profession and further increased the demand for accurate and timely communication.

**The Telegraph and Telephone:** The 19th century brought revolutionary changes in communication technology. In 1837, Samuel Morse developed the telegraph. It allowed messages to be sent over long distances using electrical signals. Messages could travel across continents in minutes instead of days.

Following this, Alexander Graham Bell invented the telephone in 1876. The telephone made it possible for people to talk to each other in real time, even if they were far apart. This transformed both personal and business communication. These inventions laid the foundation for the modern communication networks we use today.

**Radio and Television:** The 20th century introduced two major inventions that changed communication forever: radio and television. The radio allowed people to hear voices and music broadcast from a distance. It was used for entertainment, education, and even wartime communication.

Television added visuals to sound, creating a powerful medium for storytelling, news, and advertising. Both radio and TV reached millions of people and became essential parts of daily life.

They also had a major influence on culture, politics, and public opinion. Leaders could now speak directly to their citizens, and global events could be witnessed in real time.

**The Digital Age:** The late 20th century saw the rise of digital communication. Computers, email, and the internet changed the way people interacted. Information could now be stored, shared, and accessed faster than ever before. Email replaced traditional letters. Social media allowed instant updates and connections with people across the globe. Websites became sources of news, entertainment, education, and commerce.

The digital age created a global village where communication was no longer limited by geography. It became more immediate, interactive, and accessible.

**Communication in Ancient and Medieval India:** India has played a significant role in the global history of communication. India has a long and meaningful history of communication that began in ancient times. One of the earliest signs of written communication can be found in the Indus Valley Civilization, around 2600 BCE. The people of this civilization used a unique script with symbols carved on seals and pottery. Although the script has not yet been fully understood, it shows that a structured system of communication existed. Later, the Brahmi script developed around the 3rd century BCE and became the foundation for many Indian languages. Emperor Ashoka used the Brahmi script to spread messages about morality and good governance. He had these messages carved into rocks and stone pillars across his empire. Before writing became common, oral communication played a major role in India. The Vedas were passed down from generation to generation through careful memorization and chanting. These sacred texts, along with stories from the Ramayana and Mahabharata, were shared by storytellers and helped in passing on culture and values. Communication was also important in administration. Ancient texts like the Arthashastra mention the use of messengers, letters, and secret codes. During the Mughal era, communication grew stronger with organized postal services and horse riders who carried messages across regions. Important news could travel quickly between distant areas. Inscriptions on copper plates, temple walls, and stones were used to record royal orders and grants. Temples and learning centers like Nalanda were important places for knowledge sharing. They helped connect scholars, students, and travelers through discussions and debates. Visual art and religious symbols were also used to share spiritual and cultural messages. Over time, these various forms of communication helped shape Indian society. They supported learning, unity, and administration, forming a strong base for the modern systems of communication we use today.

***Section Closed...***

### *Part-3: Culture Speaks Too: How Beliefs, Values, and Traditions Influence*

Communication does not occur in isolation. It is shaped, moulded, and deeply influenced by the environment in which it takes place. Among the most powerful forces that shape communication is culture. Culture speaks through us in subtle and overt ways, influencing not only what we say but also how we say it, when we say it, and to whom. It determines the meanings behind our words, gestures, and silences. When we understand how beliefs, values, and traditions form the underlying framework of human interaction, we begin to see communication as not just a skill but a cultural expression.

Culture is not limited to regional practices or artistic expressions. It encompasses the deeply held assumptions, expectations, norms, and moral codes that individuals internalize through socialization. These cultural elements guide our interpretations and responses, thus directly impacting the messages we send and receive. When we say culture speaks too, we mean that every act of communication is, in many ways, a reflection of the cultural fabric in which it is embedded.

**Interconnection Between Culture and Communication:** Culture and communication are inseparable. One cannot exist without the other. Communication is the mechanism through which culture is transmitted, preserved, and transformed. At the same time, culture provides the context and the framework within which communication takes place. Every interaction, whether personal or public, informal or formal, carries within it the imprints of cultural influences.

From language choices to body language, from conversational styles to the interpretation of silence, culture shapes every nuance of communication. It tells us what is acceptable and what is inappropriate. It guides our judgments and expectations in both familiar and unfamiliar social settings. Without cultural context, messages can be misunderstood or misinterpreted, leading to confusion or even conflict.

Understanding this interconnection allows us to communicate more effectively across cultural boundaries. It equips us to become not just better speakers or writers, but better listeners, observers, and interpreters of human behavior.

**Beliefs as the Foundation of Cultural Messaging:** Beliefs are the deeply held convictions that individuals and groups consider to be true. These can be spiritual, philosophical, moral, or social in nature. They shape our worldview and form the internal compass by which we navigate daily life. In the realm of communication, beliefs play a powerful role in determining not only what is communicated but also how messages are constructed and interpreted.

For instance, individuals who hold a belief in collectivism may prioritize harmony, group consensus, and indirect forms of communication. On the other hand, those rooted in individualistic beliefs may value directness, self-expression, and personal opinions. These differences are not mere preferences but reflections of deep-rooted cultural belief systems.

The influence of beliefs extends to how people approach topics such as authority, gender roles, age, success, failure, and morality. These beliefs form the basis for culturally specific norms that guide communication. By becoming aware of differing belief systems, we can better navigate interactions in a multicultural world and avoid common pitfalls in cross-cultural communication.

**Role of Values in Communication Patterns:** Values represent the shared ideals that a group considers important. They are the guiding principles that define what is good, desirable, or worthwhile. While beliefs concern what people think is true, values concern what people think is right. Both are interwoven, and together they shape the framework of communication within a cultural group.

Values influence the way people prioritize their actions, their speech, and their reactions. For example, cultures that value respect for elders may discourage open disagreement with older individuals. Cultures that emphasize punctuality may interpret lateness as disrespect, while others may view time more fluidly.

The concept of politeness, honesty, modesty, and hospitality varies greatly across cultures because of differing values. These values dictate not only what people say, but also what they choose not to say. They shape the tone, intent, and delivery of messages. When values align between communicators, interactions flow smoothly. When they clash, misunderstandings can occur even when both parties speak the same language fluently.

To communicate effectively across cultures, one must understand and respect the values of others. This does not mean abandoning one's own values but being aware of how others might interpret or prioritize situations differently.

**Traditions as Expressions of Cultural Identity:** Traditions are the inherited customs and practices that are passed down from generation to generation. They are the tangible manifestations of a culture's beliefs and values. While beliefs are internal and values are philosophical, traditions are visible, practiced, and often celebrated.

In communication, traditions often dictate formalities, greetings, rituals, and ceremonies. They shape how people begin conversations, how they show respect, how they resolve conflicts, and how they celebrate milestones. For example, in some cultures, offering food or gifts before initiating a discussion is a traditional form of hospitality and goodwill. In others, starting a conversation with a firm handshake and eye contact reflects confidence and honesty.

Understanding traditions allows communicators to engage with others more meaningfully. It fosters respect and appreciation for cultural practices that may initially seem unfamiliar. Traditions also serve as powerful tools of unity, binding communities together through shared experiences and reinforcing a collective identity.

**Language as a Cultural Medium:** Language is more than a system of words and grammar. It is a cultural tool that encodes the experiences, beliefs, and worldview of its speakers. Every language carries with it unique idioms, metaphors, and expressions that reflect the history and mindset of its culture. The vocabulary available in a language often reveals what that culture values.

In some cultures, there are numerous words to describe family relationships, reflecting the importance of kinship. In others, there may be elaborate terms for nature, seasons, or emotions. The way people use language; including tone, pace, and silence that is also shaped by cultural norms.

Language becomes even more nuanced when speakers engage in cross-cultural communication. Even when people speak the same language, such as English, their cultural interpretations can lead to differences in meaning. Humor, sarcasm, formality, and politeness often vary across cultural lines. Being sensitive to these linguistic nuances is essential for respectful and effective communication.

**Non-Verbal Communication Across Cultures:** While words carry meaning, non-verbal cues often carry even more. Facial expressions, gestures, posture, eye contact, and physical distance are all part of non-verbal communication, and these elements vary widely between cultures.

In some cultures, prolonged eye contact is seen as a sign of attentiveness and respect. In others, it may be perceived as aggressive or disrespectful. A gesture that signals agreement in one culture may have a completely different or even offensive meaning in another.

Non-verbal communication often operates unconsciously, making it easy to misinterpret across cultural lines. This makes cultural awareness critical. Observing and learning about the non-verbal norms of different cultures can prevent miscommunication and foster deeper connections.

**Silence as a Cultural Statement:** Silence is not the absence of communication. In many cultures, silence carries profound meaning. It can indicate respect, contemplation, disagreement, or discomfort. The interpretation of silence varies widely depending on cultural expectations.

In some societies, silence during a conversation is welcomed and even expected as a sign of thoughtfulness or respect. In others, it may be perceived as awkward or disapproving. How individuals use and interpret silence speaks volumes about their cultural upbringing.

Understanding when and how to use silence effectively requires cultural sensitivity. Rather than fearing silence, communicators can learn to embrace it as part of the cultural dialogue, using it strategically and respectfully.

**Cultural Influence in Conflict and Resolution:** Every culture has its own way of handling conflict. Some cultures prefer direct confrontation and open discussion. Others emphasize harmony and may approach conflict indirectly, using mediation or silent withdrawal. These differences in conflict resolution styles stem from underlying beliefs, values, and traditions.

In intercultural settings, conflict can often arise not because of malice but because of differences in communication expectations. One party may view directness as honesty, while another may see it as rudeness. Misaligned expectations can escalate disagreements if cultural perspectives are not considered.

Effective conflict resolution requires more than strong communication skills. It requires empathy, cultural understanding, and the ability to see a situation from multiple viewpoints. Embracing these differences can transform conflict into an opportunity for growth and mutual understanding.

**Globalization and Cultural Communication:** The modern world is increasingly interconnected. Globalization has brought people of diverse cultural backgrounds into closer contact than ever before. This presents both opportunities and challenges for communication.

On one hand, globalization allows for greater cultural exchange, broader perspectives, and more inclusive dialogue. On the other hand, it can lead to cultural homogenization or misunderstandings when people assume their communication style is universal.

To navigate this global landscape, individuals must develop intercultural competence. This includes being open to learning about other cultures, adapting communication styles, and recognizing one's own cultural biases. In doing so, we can create more inclusive and respectful global communities.

**Cultural Intelligence in the Modern Era:** Cultural intelligence refers to the ability to relate and work effectively across cultures. It goes beyond basic knowledge of customs and requires a deeper understanding of how culture shapes communication. It involves awareness, sensitivity, and adaptability. Developing cultural intelligence is essential in today's multicultural workplaces, educational institutions, and social environments. It allows individuals to avoid stereotypes, appreciate differences, and engage with others in meaningful ways.

By investing in cultural intelligence, we are not only enhancing communication skills but also promoting empathy, cooperation, and social harmony. It is a skill that fosters unity in diversity and builds bridges between people of all backgrounds. Culture is an ever-present voice in human communication. It speaks through our beliefs, values, and traditions, shaping every message we send and receive. Whether through language, silence, gesture, or tone, culture influences the content and context of our interactions.

To communicate effectively in a diverse world, we must recognize and honor this cultural voice. We must listen with empathy, speak with respect, and engage with curiosity.

Culture speaks not only in the words we choose but in the meaning we give them. It is the invisible thread that connects us, the silent partner in every conversation, and the guiding force behind our shared human expression.

***Section Closed...***

## *Part-4: Mind Matters: Psychology Behind Communication*

Human beings are inherently social creatures. From the moment we are born, we begin to engage with the world around us through the powerful tool of communication. Yet, the act of speaking, listening, writing, or expressing is far more than a mechanical exchange of words. It is a deep psychological process influenced by our emotions, thoughts, past experiences, and cultural backgrounds. This chapter explores the psychology that shapes our communication and human connection, aiming to unveil how the mind governs the subtle yet profound ways we interact with one another.

**The Foundation of Human Communication:** Communication is often understood as the exchange of information through spoken or written language. However, psychology teaches us that true communication involves the transmission of meaning. This process is intricate, requiring the sender to encode a message in a specific format and the receiver to decode it in a way that preserves its intended meaning.

This transfer is influenced by numerous internal and external factors, including beliefs, perception, mental state, and social context. Misunderstandings often occur not because of incorrect words but due to mismatched interpretations. Our mind filters every message we send and receive, shaping how we understand and respond.

**The Role of Perception in Communication:** Perception plays a central role in shaping the way we communicate. Our senses gather information from the environment, but it is the brain that interprets this information. Two individuals can observe the same event and interpret it differently based on their prior experiences, beliefs, and psychological state.

Perceptual filters act as cognitive lenses, colouring our view of others and their messages. For instance, someone with high anxiety might perceive neutral comments as threatening, while an optimistic individual may interpret criticism as constructive. Recognizing the subjective nature of perception helps improve empathy and adaptability in our interactions.

**The Cognitive Framework of Connection:** Cognitive psychology delves into how our thoughts, memory, and reasoning processes influence communication. Before we speak or respond, we mentally process information, assess social cues, and predict outcomes. This inner mental activity is often subconscious but deeply impactful.

Schemas, or mental frameworks, are essential in this regard. They guide our expectations and responses in different social settings. These frameworks are developed through life experiences and constantly updated. When we encounter someone new, our brain draws from these schemas to evaluate how to behave or communicate. Cognitive biases also come into play, sometimes leading us to make flawed judgments that affect our relationships.

**Emotional Intelligence and Human Interaction:** Emotions are tightly interwoven with communication. Emotional intelligence, the ability to recognize, understand, manage, and influence emotions, plays a critical role in meaningful human interaction. A person with high emotional intelligence can perceive subtle emotional cues, control their reactions, and navigate conversations more effectively.

Understanding one's own emotions allows for better self-expression, while empathy enables a deeper connection with others. Emotionally intelligent individuals are often better at conflict resolution, persuasion, and leadership, primarily because they communicate with sensitivity and awareness.

**Nonverbal Communication and Its Impact:** A large part of our communication occurs without words. Facial expressions, gestures, posture, eye contact, and tone of voice communicate volumes about our thoughts and feelings. In fact, research suggests that nonverbal cues can often convey more authenticity than spoken words.

The psychology behind nonverbal communication shows that much of this expression is instinctive and driven by the limbic system, the brain's emotional centre. When someone fakes a smile, for example, micro-expressions often reveal the truth. Recognizing and interpreting nonverbal signals requires attentiveness and psychological insight, but doing so significantly enhances interpersonal understanding.

**Language, Thought, and Culture:** The relationship between language and thought has fascinated psychologists and linguists for centuries. Language is not merely a means of expression but also a framework through which we structure our thoughts. The words we choose reflect how we perceive reality.

Different languages emphasize different aspects of experience. For example, some languages have multiple words for concepts that other languages capture in a single term.

This linguistic relativity shapes not only how we communicate but how we perceive time, space, relationships, and emotions.

Culture, too, plays a significant role. Cultural norms dictate what is considered polite, assertive, or inappropriate. In some cultures, direct communication is valued, while in others, indirectness is preferred. Understanding the psychological underpinnings of cross-cultural communication is vital in an increasingly interconnected world.

**The Social Brain: How We Bond and Belong:** Neuroscience has revealed that our brains are wired for connection. The human brain contains specialized regions responsible for social cognition. These areas allow us to read others' emotions, understand intentions, and develop a sense of belonging.

One key concept is the mirror neuron system, which activates both when we perform an action and when we observe someone else performing the same action. This system is believed to be crucial for empathy, imitation, and learning social behaviors.

Attachment theory also provides insight into how early relationships shape our communication patterns. People with secure attachment styles tend to be more open and trusting in conversations, while those with insecure attachments may struggle with vulnerability or conflict. Our need to connect and feel accepted influences how we communicate in every relationship.

**Psychological Barriers to Effective Communication:** Despite our inherent capacity for connection, various psychological barriers can hinder communication. These include anxiety, fear of judgment, low self-esteem, and cognitive distortions such as all-or-nothing thinking or catastrophizing.

Stress and trauma can also affect communication. Individuals who have experienced emotional trauma may find it difficult to trust, express emotions, or interpret others' intentions accurately. Their minds are often in a heightened state of alert, which can cause defensiveness or withdrawal.

Recognizing and addressing these barriers is crucial for developing healthy communication habits. Therapy, self-awareness, and supportive environments can help individuals overcome these hurdles and foster more meaningful connections.

**The Psychology of Listening:** Listening is a powerful yet underappreciated aspect of communication. Psychological studies show that active listening not only improves understanding but also strengthens relationships. Active listeners focus their attention, minimize distractions, and respond with empathy and validation.

Barriers to listening include preconceived judgments, distraction, emotional reactivity, and the tendency to formulate a reply before the other person has finished speaking. True listening requires patience and presence. It is a skill that can be cultivated through mindfulness and intentionality.

Moreover, listening satisfies a deep psychological need to be seen and heard. When people feel listened to, they experience a sense of validation and connection that goes beyond words.

**Digital Communication and the Modern Mind:** In the digital age, communication has evolved dramatically. Text messages, emails, video calls, and social media have transformed the way we connect. While these tools offer convenience and global reach, they also introduce psychological challenges. The absence of nonverbal cues in digital communication can lead to misinterpretation. Tone, intent, and emotion may be unclear, increasing the likelihood of conflict. Social media, in particular, creates curated realities that influence self-esteem and interpersonal dynamics.

Yet digital platforms also serve as outlets for expression, especially for those who struggle with face-to-face interactions. The psychology of online communication is still emerging, but it is clear that the human need for connection remains central, regardless of the medium.

**Power Dynamics and Psychological Influence:** Communication is not always a neutral exchange. Power dynamics often shape how and what people communicate. In professional, familial, or social hierarchies, the psychological presence of authority or submission influences tone, language, and openness. The psychology of persuasion and influence further highlights how communication can shape behavior and belief. Techniques such as framing, storytelling, repetition, and appeals to emotion are used to guide or shift perspectives.

**Identity, Self-Concept, and Expression:** The way we communicate is an extension of how we see ourselves. Self-concept, formed through internal beliefs and social feedback, influences our confidence, assertiveness, and clarity in communication. People with a strong, positive self-concept tend to express themselves more authentically and constructively. Communication also serves as a tool for identity formation. Through conversation and expression, individuals test ideas, refine values, and solidify roles. This is especially evident during adolescence and other transitional phases of life. The act of being heard helps individuals understand who they are and what they stand for.

**The Healing Power of Communication:** Psychological research supports the idea that communication can be profoundly healing. Talking about emotions, especially in safe environments, can reduce psychological distress, build resilience, and foster emotional growth. Therapeutic conversations, whether in professional counselling or trusted relationships, allow individuals to release pent-up emotions, reframe experiences, and gain new insights. Validation and empathy received through dialogue can be transformative.

Journaling, a form of intrapersonal communication, also offers psychological benefits. Writing thoughts and feelings down helps organize the mind, reduce anxiety, and clarify goals.

**Better Communication Through Self-Awareness:** Improving communication starts with understanding the self. Self-awareness is the foundation of psychological growth and relational harmony. When individuals are aware of their emotional triggers, thought patterns, and communication styles, they can engage more intentionally and compassionately with others. Self-reflection, mindfulness, and feedback from others are valuable tools in developing self-awareness. It is a continual process, one that deepens with experience and willingness to grow.

By cultivating self-awareness, individuals can become more adaptive, empathetic, and clear in their communication, thereby enriching their personal and professional relationships.

The psychology of communication reveals that our words, actions, and expressions are not isolated behaviours but reflections of complex mental processes. Human connection is not merely about exchanging ideas but about understanding, empathy, and emotional resonance. Whether through a comforting conversation, a heartfelt letter, or a quiet presence, the mind seeks to connect with others in meaningful ways.

Understanding the psychology behind how we communicate and connect allows us to navigate relationships with more grace, build trust with more integrity, and listen with more depth. Communication is not just a skill but a reflection of the inner world, shaped by the mind's intricate architecture and its yearning for connection. As we deepen our psychological understanding of communication, we uncover not only better ways to interact but richer ways to live.

***Section Closed...***

### *Part-5: Communication: Empowering Expression*

Communication is the process by which people exchange ideas, information, thoughts, and emotions. It plays a vital role in every aspect of human life, from personal relationships to professional settings. Without communication, there would be no way to express thoughts, share knowledge, or build understanding.

At its core, communication is about connecting people. It allows individuals to convey their intentions, feelings, and thoughts clearly to others. Whether it is speaking to a friend, writing an email, or delivering a speech to a large audience, communication is the bridge that links individuals and groups.

**Definition of Communication:** Communication is the act of transferring information from one person, group, or place to another. It can be spoken, written, visual, or non-verbal. The key goal of communication is to ensure that the message is understood by the receiver as intended by the sender.

In simple terms, communication is the process through which a sender conveys a message to a receiver, and the receiver provides feedback to show understanding. This continuous process is essential for cooperation, collaboration, and productivity in various environments such as homes, schools, workplaces, and society.

**Process of Communication:** The communication process involves a series of steps that ensure the proper transfer and understanding of a message. These steps can be explained as follows:

**(i) Sender:** The sender is the person who initiates the message. The sender decides what message to convey and chooses the way to deliver it. This may include thinking about how to say something and selecting the most appropriate channel.

**(ii) Encoding:** Encoding is the process of turning thoughts into communication. This may include forming words, writing messages, creating gestures, or using visuals. The quality of encoding depends on the sender's clarity of thought and the medium chosen.

**(iii) Message:** The message is the actual content that is being communicated. It may be an idea, instruction, opinion, or feeling. A message must be clear and structured for effective communication.

**(iv) Channel:** The channel is the medium through which the message is sent. It can be spoken, written, or sent through electronic means like email or video. The choice of the channel depends on the situation and urgency of the message.

**(v) Receiver:** The receiver is the person or group for whom the message is intended. The receiver must correctly interpret and understand the message.

**(vi) Decoding:** Decoding is the process through which the receiver interprets the message. It involves understanding the meaning of words, tone, body language, and other elements. Effective communication occurs when the receiver's interpretation matches the sender's intent.

**(vii) Feedback:** Feedback is the response from the receiver to the sender. It helps the sender know whether the message was understood correctly.

**Importance of Communication:** Communication is essential in every field of life. It helps to build relationships, solve problems, make decisions, and share knowledge. The following points highlight the importance of communication:

Communication helps in expressing feelings and emotions effectively.

It builds trust and transparency in relationships, whether personal or professional.

It supports teamwork and collaboration by promoting understanding and cooperation.

It aids in decision-making through the clear exchange of information.

In the workplace, communication ensures smooth operations and improves efficiency.

In education, communication supports learning and the sharing of ideas.

It plays a key role in leadership and management by guiding, inspiring teams.

**Types of Communication:** Communication can take various forms depending on how it is delivered and the context in which it is used. The two main classifications are based on the mode of expression and the level of formality.

**Verbal and Non-Verbal Communication:** Verbal and non-verbal communication are the two basic ways people express themselves.

**(i) Verbal Communication:** Verbal communication involves the use of spoken or written words to convey a message. It includes face-to-face conversations, telephone calls, video chats, speeches, presentations, and written messages such as letters, emails, and texts.

Effective verbal communication requires clarity, correct grammar, tone, and confidence. It is important to use the right words and ensure the message is structured and understandable.

**(ii) Non-Verbal Communication:** Non-verbal communication includes body language, facial expressions, gestures, posture, eye contact, tone of voice, and even silence. It often conveys emotions and attitudes more effectively than words.

For example, a smile may express friendliness, while crossed arms might show defensiveness. Even the tone in which something is said can change the meaning of the message. Non-verbal communication supports verbal communication by adding depth and meaning. However, it can also create confusion if not aligned with the spoken words.

**Formal and Informal Communication:** This classification is based on the level of structure and professionalism.

**(i) Formal Communication:** Formal communication follows a defined structure and is used in professional settings. It occurs within the official hierarchy of organizations and follows rules and protocols.

Examples include business meetings, official emails, reports, notices, and presentations. Formal communication ensures discipline, clarity, and accountability.

**(ii) Informal Communication:** Informal communication is casual and spontaneous. It occurs naturally among friends, colleagues, or family members. This type of communication does not follow any set rules and is often more relaxed.

Informal communication helps build personal bonds and can improve workplace morale and relationships. However, it must be used carefully in professional environments to avoid misunderstandings.

**Barriers to Communication and Overcoming Them:** Communication is not always smooth. Various barriers can distort the message, cause misunderstanding, or lead to conflict. Identifying and overcoming these barriers is essential for effective communication.

**(i) Physical Barriers:** Physical barriers include distance, noise, poor internet connection, or a lack of privacy. These obstacles make it difficult to hear or focus on the message.

**(ii) Language Barriers:** Language differences, jargon, unfamiliar accents, and complex vocabulary can prevent the receiver from understanding the message.

**(iv) Emotional Barriers:** Fear, anger, anxiety, or lack of confidence can stop someone from communicating effectively. Emotions may also affect how a message is received.

**(v) Cultural Barriers:** Differences in culture, values, and beliefs can lead to misunderstandings. What is acceptable in one culture may be offensive in another.

**(vi) Perceptual Barriers:** Perception is how people interpret information. Personal bias, stereotypes, and assumptions can lead to misinterpretation of messages.

**(vii) Organizational Barriers:** In large organizations, hierarchical levels and complex structures may delay or distort communication. Poor coordination and unclear policies can also create confusion.

**(viii) Technological Barriers:** Dependence on digital tools may cause issues when there is a lack of access, skills, or system failures. Misuse of technology may also affect communication tone.

**7Cs of Effective Communication:** The 7Cs are the essential principles that help improve the effectiveness of communication. These guidelines ensure that the message is clear, concise, and impactful.

**(i) Clarity:** Clarity means the message should be clear and easy to understand. Avoid confusion by using simple language and well-structured sentences. Be specific about what you want to say.

**(ii) Conciseness:** Conciseness involves saying what needs to be said in as few words as possible. Avoid unnecessary words or repeated ideas.

**(iii) Correctness:** Correctness refers to the use of accurate language, grammar, and facts. A correct message creates credibility and prevents misunderstandings. It also includes choosing the right tone for the audience.

**(iv) Completeness:** A complete message contains all the necessary information. It answers all questions and provides relevant details so that the receiver can understand and take action if needed.

**(v) Consideration:** Consideration means understanding the audience's needs, background, and perspective. Choose words and examples that match their level of understanding and show respect for their views.

**(vi) Concreteness:** Concreteness involves using specific facts and examples instead of vague or general language. A concrete message is strong, convincing, and easier to remember.

**(vii) Courtesy:** Courtesy is about being respectful, polite, and positive in communication. Even when disagreeing or delivering criticism, it is important to maintain a respectful tone.

Communication is the foundation of human interaction. It connects people, ideas, and emotions across all aspects of life. Understanding the communication process and the types involved helps individuals interact more effectively in different settings.

Overcoming communication barriers and following the principles of the 7Cs can improve the quality of both personal and professional relationships. Good communication is not just about speaking well but also about listening, understanding, and responding appropriately.

Whether in a family, workplace, educational institution, or society at large, effective communication remains a key skill that leads to success, growth, and harmony.

****

# CHAPTER – II : THE WORKPLACE LENS

*Professional Communication in Organizational Settings*

## *Part-1: Inside the Organization: Psychology, Behaviour, and Communication*

Organizations are more than just structured entities where tasks are assigned, goals are pursued, and profits are earned. They are dynamic ecosystems powered by the psychological mechanisms, behaviors, and communication styles of the individuals who work within them. The human aspect of professional environments significantly shapes outcomes, productivity, collaboration, and the overall atmosphere of a workplace. This chapter delves into the psychological underpinnings of workplace behavior, the nuanced ways professionals communicate, and the intricate dynamics that influence functioning within an organizational setup.

**The Psychological Framework of Organizational Life:** At the core of every organization lies a psychological landscape that determines how people think, feel, and act in professional settings. This psychological framework is influenced by individual personalities, emotional intelligence, cognitive biases, motivational drives, group dynamics. These elements contribute to both the strengths and vulnerabilities of the organization.

Workplace psychology encompasses the study of how people interact with one another, how leadership affects morale, and how workplace structures support or hinder mental well-being. When organizations understand the psychological needs of their employees, they can design strategies that foster motivation, engagement, and satisfaction.

**Understanding Behavior in the Workplace:** Behavior in the professional space is a reflection of both internal factors and external stimuli. While personality traits influence how individuals approach their work, environmental conditions such as workload, team dynamics, and organizational culture also play a critical role.

Employees bring their values, attitudes, and belief systems into the workplace. These elements interact with organizational policies, leadership styles, and workplace culture to shape behavior. For example, a supportive environment can enhance cooperation and trust, while a toxic one may breed defensiveness and withdrawal. Organizational behavior, as a field of study, helps leaders and managers understand these patterns and intervene in ways that promote positive outcomes. Recognizing behavioral trends early allows for timely adjustments that preserve morale and performance.

**Emotional Intelligence and Its Role in the Professional (Workplace) Spaces:** Emotional intelligence is the ability to perceive, understand, and manage emotions both within oneself and in others. In the workplace, this ability is crucial for effective communication, collaboration, and leadership. An emotionally intelligent employee can navigate conflict, adapt to change, and empathize with colleagues.

Professionals with high emotional intelligence contribute to a positive workplace culture. They are often better at regulating their responses, offering support, and maintaining constructive relationships. These traits are not only essential for personal success but also for maintaining organizational harmony.

Managers and leaders who demonstrate emotional intelligence are more capable of building trust, inspiring teams, and fostering inclusive environments. Organizations that prioritize emotional intelligence in recruitment and training benefit from stronger interpersonal dynamics and resilience.

**The Impact of Motivation and Job Satisfaction:** Motivation is a psychological force that directs behavior toward specific goals. In organizational settings, understanding what motivates employees is key to improving performance and satisfaction. Motivation can be intrinsic, stemming from internal rewards such as personal growth or a sense of purpose, or extrinsic, driven by external factors like pay, recognition, or job security.

Job satisfaction arises when an employee's expectations align with their work experience. It is influenced by factors such as workload, autonomy, relationships, and opportunities for advancement. High job satisfaction contributes to reduced turnover, increased productivity, and a stronger organizational reputation.

Leaders who invest in understanding what drives their teams are better positioned to create an environment where people feel valued and motivated. This psychological insight helps to align individual aspirations with organizational objectives.

**Organizational Culture & Psychological Safety:** Organizational culture encompasses the shared values, norms, and practices that shape how things are done within a workplace. Culture is not always consciously designed but evolves over time through collective behavior and leadership influence.

One of the most important aspects of a healthy organizational culture is psychological safety. This is the belief that one can speak up, take risks, or admit mistakes without fear of punishment or humiliation. Psychological safety encourages innovation, collaboration, and honest dialogue. When employees feel safe and supported, they are more likely to contribute creative ideas, offer feedback, and engage fully in their roles. Conversely, a culture marked by fear or rigidity stifles growth and creates barriers to communication.

Fostering a psychologically safe culture involves active listening, nonjudgmental communication, and modeling respectful behavior from leadership down to entry-level positions.

**Leadership Psychology and Influence:** The psychology of leadership is a complex field that examines how individuals inspire, influence, and guide others within an organization. Effective leadership is not based solely on authority or technical skill but on the ability to understand people and connect with them authentically.

Transformational leaders, who motivate others by aligning organizational vision with personal values, often have a deep understanding of psychological principles. They build trust through transparency, encourage development, and empower their teams.

Leadership behavior sets the tone for the entire organization. A leader who demonstrates empathy, consistency, and ethical conduct creates an atmosphere of trust and reliability. On the other hand, autocratic or erratic leadership can lead to confusion, resistance, and disengagement. Understanding leadership psychology enables organizations to develop leaders who are not only competent but also capable of nurturing human potential.

**Communication as a Psychological Process:** Communication in professional settings is far more than the exchange of information. It is a psychological process shaped by perception, cognition, emotion, and social context. Effective communication requires clarity, empathy, and attentiveness to both verbal and nonverbal cues. The way messages are framed can significantly impact how they are received. A directive delivered with empathy tends to be more effective than one conveyed with impatience. Miscommunication often arises not from poor language but from mismatched interpretations rooted in psychological states.

Listening is equally important as speaking. Active listening involves giving full attention, withholding judgment, and responding thoughtfully. It builds trust and allows for deeper understanding. Communication also involves managing conflict, providing feedback, and creating opportunities for dialogue. These interactions are more successful when approached with emotional awareness and psychological insight.

**Group Dynamics and Team Behaviour:** Within any organization, individuals are rarely isolated. They operate within teams, departments, and collaborative networks. Group dynamics play a crucial role in shaping behavior and outcomes.

Teams that function well typically have clear roles, shared goals, and open communication. However, groups can also fall prey to dysfunctional patterns such as groupthink, social loafing, or dominance by a few voices. Understanding the psychological principles behind group behavior helps in designing teams that are productive and harmonious. Interpersonal relationships within teams are affected by trust, respect, and the ability to manage differences. Diversity in thought and background can enhance creativity, but only when differences are embraced and managed constructively.

Facilitating positive group dynamics requires attention to team structure, communication patterns, and the emotional climate. When done effectively, teamwork becomes a source of energy and innovation.

**Conflict and Resolution in Professional Environments:** Conflict is inevitable in any organization, arising from differences in opinion, goals, or values. While often seen as negative, conflict can be an opportunity for growth and improvement when managed properly. The psychological response to conflict varies from person to person. Some may become defensive, while others may avoid confrontation entirely. Understanding these tendencies helps in navigating conflict with greater effectiveness.

Resolution involves more than compromise. It requires empathy, open dialogue, and a willingness to find common ground. Mediating conflict successfully relies on communication skills, emotional regulation, and a mindset oriented toward collaboration. Organizations that train their staff in conflict resolution benefit from fewer disruptions, stronger relationships, and a culture of mutual respect.

**Change and Psychological Adaptation:** Organizational change is a constant in the modern workplace. Whether through restructuring, technological upgrades, or shifts in policy, change often disrupts the familiar and challenges psychological stability. People react to change based on their tolerance for uncertainty, prior experiences, and level of involvement in the change process. Resistance often stems from fear, loss of control, or perceived threat to competence.

Facilitating change effectively involves addressing psychological concerns. Transparent communication, participation in decision-making, and access to support can ease the transition and foster buy-in. Psychological adaptation to change is a process that requires time and reassurance. When handled with sensitivity, change becomes a source of renewal rather than disruption.

**The Role of Feedback and Recognition:** Feedback is a vital communication tool that guides behavior, improves performance, and fosters professional growth. Psychologically, feedback provides information about how one's actions are perceived and whether they align with expectations. Constructive feedback is specific, timely, and delivered with empathy. It focuses on behavior rather than personality and provides a path for improvement. Poorly delivered feedback, on the other hand, can harm self-esteem and create defensiveness.

Recognition, whether formal or informal, fulfils the human need for validation and belonging. It reinforces positive behavior and contributes to job satisfaction. A culture of appreciation enhances morale and strengthens organizational commitment.

**Workplace Stress and Mental Well-being:** The psychological demands of modern work environments often lead to stress, burnout, and emotional fatigue. Deadlines, expectations, interpersonal tensions, and lack of autonomy contribute to mental strain. Chronic stress affects not only individual well-being but also organizational effectiveness. It reduces focus, increases absenteeism, and erodes workplace relationships. Addressing workplace stress requires both individual strategies and systemic changes. Organizations that prioritize mental health through policies, resources, and a supportive culture create more sustainable work environments. Encouraging work-life balance, offering flexibility, and fostering open conversations about mental health are steps toward a psychologically healthy workplace.

**Ethics, Values, and Organizational Integrity:** Every organization operates within a moral framework, whether explicitly stated or implicitly understood. Ethics in communication and behavior is a reflection of this framework. Integrity involves aligning actions with core values and maintaining consistency between what is said and done. Ethical lapses in professional settings often stem from psychological pressures such as fear of failure, desire for approval, or loyalty to authority. Cultivating a strong ethical culture requires clarity of values, ethical leadership, and systems of accountability. When individuals feel that their organization operates with fairness and honesty, trust flourishes.

The world inside an organization is a rich tapestry woven with psychological threads. From leadership to teamwork, from conflict resolution to motivation, psychology provides the tools to navigate the complex human terrain of professional life. As organizations continue to evolve, so too must their understanding of the people who bring them to life. When workplaces align with psychological insight and behavioural understanding, they become more than just places of work. They become communities where people grow, thrive, and contribute meaningfully to a shared purpose.

***Section Closed...***

## *Part-2: Talk Like a Professional: Workplace Etiquette, Feedback, and Clarity*

Professional communication is a skill that can shape the course of a person's career. In the modern workplace, how you express your thoughts, respond to others, and carry yourself during conversations matters as much as your technical skills or qualifications. Whether you are a new employee or an experienced leader, the ability to communicate with respect, clarity, and confidence defines your presence in a professional space.

This chapter explores how to talk like a professional by mastering the essentials of workplace etiquette, understanding how to give and receive feedback, and learning to communicate with clarity. These elements contribute to building a culture of respect, trust, and efficiency at work.

**Understanding Workplace Etiquette:** Workplace etiquette refers to the expected behavior and communication style that helps create a respectful and smooth-flowing environment. It includes everything from how you greet colleagues to how you send emails. Etiquette sets the tone for interactions and helps avoid misunderstandings or conflicts.

Simple gestures like saying good morning, listening when others speak, or maintaining appropriate body language show that you are respectful and aware of your surroundings. These small actions, when practiced consistently, reflect professionalism and maturity.

In a diverse work environment, etiquette also includes being sensitive to different cultures, communication styles, and personal boundaries. Professionals who adapt well to these differences are more likely to build positive relationships and thrive in team settings.

**The Power of First Impressions:** The first few seconds of a conversation or meeting can create a lasting impression. How you present yourself, your tone of voice, and your body language all play a role. A professional greeting, a confident smile, and attentive listening can make you appear approachable and trustworthy.

People often remember how they felt during their first interaction with you. Making a positive impression helps set the stage for cooperation and mutual respect. Whether you are meeting a client, a colleague, or a supervisor, your professionalism during those early moments can open doors for future collaboration.

**Speaking with Respect and Tact:** Professional communication requires you to express your thoughts clearly while being respectful to others. This means avoiding aggressive language, interrupting others, or using sarcasm. It also means being mindful of how your words might affect someone emotionally or mentally.

Using polite phrases such as "please," "thank you," or "may I" adds a tone of humility to your words. Even when discussing sensitive topics or disagreements, using a calm and respectful approach helps to maintain harmony and mutual respect.

Tact involves choosing the right words at the right time. For example, pointing out an error during a team meeting may not be appropriate unless handled delicately. Knowing when and how to speak ensures that your message is received without creating discomfort or defensiveness.

**Listening as a Professional Skill:** Listening is one of the most underrated communication skills in the workplace. Many people focus on what to say next rather than truly understanding what the other person is saying. Active listening shows that you value the other person's thoughts and are genuinely interested in their perspective.

Active listening includes maintaining eye contact, nodding occasionally to show engagement, and summarizing what the other person said to confirm understanding. Avoid distractions during conversations, such as checking your phone or typing on your computer, as this may appear disrespectful.

Good listeners are often trusted more, respected more, and approached more frequently for advice and collaboration. Listening well helps in avoiding miscommunication and strengthens workplace relationships.

**Email and Digital Communication Etiquette:** In modern offices, a large part of professional communication happens through emails, messaging platforms, or video calls. How you write and respond to digital messages reflects your professionalism and attention to detail. Emails should be clear, concise, and polite. Begin with a greeting and close with a signature or thank you. Avoid writing in all capital letters, using too many exclamation points, or being overly casual unless the relationship with the receiver allows for it.

When using messaging platforms, remember that tone can be misunderstood. What seems like a quick joke or informal comment can be misread. Always aim for clarity and kindness, especially when communicating across different time zones or cultures. During video meetings, maintain a clean background, dress appropriately, and ensure good lighting and sound. Mute your microphone when not speaking, and avoid interrupting others.

**Role of Nonverbal Communication:** Nonverbal communication includes body language, facial expressions, gestures, and posture. It plays a powerful role in how your message is received. A friendly smile, an open posture, and steady eye contact can build trust, while crossed arms, fidgeting, or lack of eye contact may signal disinterest or discomfort. Be aware of your nonverbal cues when you are speaking and when you are listening. They should match the tone and content of your words. For instance, saying "I'm open to feedback" while appearing closed off or defensive sends mixed signals. Understanding others' nonverbal cues is equally important. It helps in sensing when someone is confused, stressed, or uninterested, which allows you to adjust your message or approach accordingly.

**Giving Feedback Effectively:** Feedback is essential for growth and improvement in the workplace. Giving it properly is a professional skill that requires honesty, empathy, and clarity. Effective feedback is constructive, timely, and specific.

When giving feedback, focus on the behavior or outcome, not the person. Instead of saying "You are careless," say "I noticed there were a few errors in the report that need correcting." This keeps the conversation professional and objective.

Choose the right setting for feedback. Private matters should be discussed privately, while praise can often be shared publicly. Keep your tone calm, avoid blame, and offer suggestions for improvement.

Giving feedback should always be a two-way process. Allow the other person to share their thoughts or explain their actions. This encourages openness and a stronger sense of teamwork.

**Receiving Feedback with Grace:** Receiving feedback, especially critical feedback, can be uncomfortable. However, how you respond to feedback shows your maturity and willingness to grow. Professionals do not take feedback personally but use it as a tool for improvement.

Listen to feedback without interrupting. If you disagree, take a moment before responding. Ask questions if the feedback is unclear and thank the person for sharing their observations. Avoid becoming defensive or emotional. Even if the feedback is poorly delivered, try to extract the useful parts. Not all feedback is accurate, but it can still provide insight into how others perceive your work or behavior. Learning to handle feedback with grace improves your performance, strengthens your relationships, and shows that you are open to growth.

**Communicating with Clarity and Simplicity:** Clear communication saves time, reduces confusion, and helps achieve goals faster. Professionals who speak clearly and simply are more likely to be understood and trusted. To communicate with clarity, organize your thoughts before speaking or writing. Use simple words and short sentences. Avoid jargon unless you are sure your audience understands it. Be direct, but polite.

When giving instructions or updates, be specific about what is expected, when it is due, and who is responsible. Repeating important points or summarizing them at the end can help ensure understanding.

Ask for feedback on your message. A simple "Does that make sense?" or "Would you like me to explain it again?" shows that you care about clarity and that you respect the listener.

**Managing Difficult Conversations:** Difficult conversations are a part of professional life. These can include delivering bad news, addressing a performance issue, or discussing conflicts. Professionals approach these conversations with preparation, patience, and empathy. Start by identifying the purpose of the conversation. Stick to facts, avoid emotional language, and stay calm. Use a respectful tone and listen to the other person's side of the story. Give them space to express themselves. It helps to focus on solutions rather than blame. Discuss what can be done to resolve the issue or improve the situation. End the conversation with clarity about the next steps or agreements made. Managing difficult conversations professionally builds trust, shows leadership, and prevents small issues from becoming bigger problems.

**Set Professional Boundaries:** Professional communication also involves setting and respecting boundaries. This includes understanding what is appropriate to discuss at work, when to share personal opinions, and how to manage workplace relationships. Avoid gossip, sensitive topics, or negative remarks about others. Keep conversations respectful, even when discussing personal matters. Respect your colleagues' time and space, and avoid oversharing.

Boundaries help create a healthy work culture where people feel safe, respected, and focused. They also reduce the chances of conflicts, misunderstandings, or workplace discomfort. When someone crosses your boundaries, express your concerns politely and firmly. Learning to say no or request changes respectfully is a key part of professional communication.

**Building a Culture of Open Communication:** In workplaces where open communication is encouraged, employees feel more valued, engaged, and productive. Openness does not mean sharing everything. It means that people feel comfortable expressing ideas, asking questions, and raising concerns without fear.

Leaders play a big role in setting tone for open communication. By being transparent, approachable, and respectful, they create an environment where honesty and collaboration thrive. Encourage regular check-ins, team discussions, and feedback sessions. Provide opportunities for employees to contribute to decisions or voice their opinions. Celebrate diverse ideas and listen to different perspectives. When communication flows freely and respectfully, organizations become more adaptive, creative, and united.

Professional communication brings out the best in individuals and teams. It reduces conflict, strengthens trust, and improves performance. It also reflects who we are as professionals and how we value the people around us.

By practicing the principles in this chapter, you will not only talk like a professional but also think, act, and lead with professionalism. In doing so, you contribute to a workplace culture that is respectful, inclusive, and effective.

***Section Closed...***

## *Part-3: Beyond Words: Handling Misunderstandings, Conflicts and Communication Breakdown*

Communication is often considered the foundation of all human interaction. In professional environments, how we communicate can either build strong relationships or create tension. However, no matter how skilled we are, misunderstandings, conflicts, and breakdowns in communication are sometimes unavoidable. These situations can affect trust, teamwork, and productivity. Knowing how to handle them with maturity and professionalism is a key trait of effective leaders and responsible professionals.

This chapter focuses on the delicate yet essential aspects of workplace communication. It explores why misunderstandings happen, how to deal with conflicts constructively, and what to do when communication fails. By learning how to navigate these challenges, individuals can build more respectful, cooperative, and emotionally intelligent workplaces.

**Understanding Misunderstandings:** A misunderstanding occurs when one person misinterprets what another person is trying to say. This can be due to unclear language, poor listening, assumptions, or emotional reactions. In fast-paced workplaces where people communicate through multiple channels, such as emails, chats, and meetings, the chances of miscommunication increase. Sometimes, what is said is not what is heard. Even a small change in tone or wording can lead to confusion. For example, a brief email response may seem rude to one person but neutral to another. A joke in a team meeting might be taken lightly by some but offend others. Misunderstandings can affect work output, damage relationships, or create emotional discomfort. Recognizing that they are a normal part of human interaction is the first step to addressing them. The goal is not to avoid all misunderstandings but to become skilled in identifying and resolving them early.

**The Role of Assumptions and Expectations:** One of the most common causes of all misunderstandings is assuming that others know what we mean or expect. We often communicate based on our personal background, culture, or experience, and forget that others may not share the same context.

In professional spaces, unclear expectations about roles, responsibilities, or deadlines can lead to tension. For example, if a manager assumes that a task should be completed by Friday without clearly stating it, and the employee believes the deadline is Monday, this creates a problem. Setting clear expectations, confirming understanding, and asking clarifying questions can help reduce the chances of miscommunication. It is better to overcommunicate slightly than to leave things open to interpretation.

**Listening to Understand:** Listening is more than just hearing words. It is about being present, showing interest, and trying to understand the other person's point of view. When people do not feel heard, they become frustrated or defensive, which can lead to conflict. Active listening involves making eye contact, allowing the speaker to finish, and responding thoughtfully. It also includes listening without preparing your response while the other person is still speaking. Many communication problems can be avoided by simply listening more attentively. When we listen to understand rather than to reply, we reduce the chances of assumptions and allow space for clarity.

**Managing Emotions in Communication:** Emotions are deeply tied to communication. When people are stressed, tired, or frustrated, they may say things they do not mean or interpret others' words more negatively than intended.

Professionals must be aware of their emotional state when communicating. Speaking while angry or anxious can lead to regret later. Similarly, being too emotional when receiving feedback or criticism can result in misunderstandings or hurt feelings. Taking a moment to breathe, pause, or step away before responding in emotionally charged situations can prevent conflicts from escalating. Emotional self-awareness helps individuals communicate with more calmness, compassion, and clarity.

**Handling Conflicts Professionally:** Conflict is not always negative. It can lead to growth, innovation, and better understanding when managed correctly. However, many people fear conflict or try to avoid it entirely. Ignoring issues can cause resentment and damage team dynamics. Handling conflict professionally means addressing the issue directly but respectfully. It involves discussing facts rather than making personal judgments. For instance, saying "I noticed that the deadline was missed" is more effective than saying "You are always late with your work."

Both parties should be given a chance to speak and explain their perspective. The goal is not to win an argument but to find a solution that respects everyone involved. A calm tone, respectful language, and willingness to compromise are key elements of successful conflict resolution.

**Conflict from Cultural and Communication Style Differences:** Workplaces today are often made up of individuals from different cultures, backgrounds, and communication styles. What is considered polite or normal in one culture may seem rude or confusing in another. These differences can lead to unintended conflicts or misunderstandings. Some people prefer direct communication, while others are more indirect. Some value personal relationships at work, while others focus strictly on tasks. Understanding these differences and approaching them with curiosity rather than judgment can help prevent tension. Professionals should strive to be culturally aware and respectful. Asking questions, avoiding assumptions, and being open-minded helps create a more inclusive environment where people feel safe to express themselves.

**Dealing with Communication Breakdowns:** Sometimes, communication breaks down completely. Messages are not delivered, misunderstandings continue to grow, and relationships become strained. In such cases, a proactive approach is needed to restore clarity and trust. The first step is to identify the source of the breakdown. Is it a lack of clarity? A lack of follow-up? Emotional tension? Once the root issue is identified, it becomes easier to address it.

It may help to restart the conversation from the beginning, using simple and clear language. Asking the other person what they understood and comparing it with what was intended can bring clarity. A third person, such as a manager or HR representative, may be needed to mediate the situation if emotions are high. Restoring broken communication requires humility, patience, and the willingness to make things right rather than prove a point.

**Building a Culture of Open Dialogue:** One of the most effective ways to prevent communication problems is to create a culture where open and honest dialogue is encouraged. When employees feel safe to speak up, ask questions, or admit confusion, misunderstandings are less likely to turn into conflicts.

Leaders play a big role in setting this tone. By being approachable, transparent, and responsive, they show that communication is a shared responsibility. Teams that regularly check in, discuss challenges, and provide feedback openly tend to work more smoothly together. Encouraging open dialogue also means accepting that mistakes will happen. The focus should be on learning and improving communication over time, not on blaming or punishing others.

**Apologizing and Repairing Relationships:** Sometimes, we may unintentionally say or do something that causes hurt or confusion. Owning up to it, apologizing sincerely, and making an effort to repair the relationship is a strong sign of professionalism and emotional maturity.

An apology should not be vague or defensive. Instead of saying "Sorry if you were offended," a better approach is "I realize my comment may have upset you, and I truly regret that. It was not my intention." This shows responsibility and care.

Rebuilding trust after a communication mistake takes time, but sincere effort and consistent behavior can restore respect and collaboration.

**Using the Technology Thoughtfully:** In today's workplaces, communication happens through many platforms such as email, messaging apps, and video calls. While these tools are useful, they also come with risks for miscommunication. Tone is often lost in text-based messages. A simple message may appear cold or angry when that was not the sender's intention. Misreading emojis or abbreviations can also cause confusion.

When discussing sensitive topics or resolving misunderstandings, it is better to talk in person or through a video call rather than messaging. Hearing someone's voice or seeing their facial expressions adds a layer of understanding that text cannot provide. Professionals should also be careful about their response time. Ignoring messages for too long, sending messages at inappropriate hours, or writing without proper punctuation can lead to misunderstandings.

**Preventing Communication Challenges through Clarity:** The best way to prevent communication challenges is to be as clear and transparent as possible from the start. Whether you are giving instructions, delegating tasks, or offering feedback, aim for simplicity and precision. Check if the other person has understood you correctly. This can be done by asking them to repeat or summarize the key points. Encourage questions and keep the lines of communication open throughout the process.

Clarity also means being honest about what you can and cannot do. If you need more time, do not promise something you cannot deliver. If you do not understand something, ask for clarification instead of pretending. Over time, people will respect you more for your honesty, clarity, and effort to communicate effectively.

**Emotional Intelligence and Communication:** Emotional intelligence is the ability to understand and manage your emotions and those of others. It is closely connected with effective communication. People with high emotional intelligence are better at resolving conflicts, handling misunderstandings, and calming tense situations.

They do not just react to what others say. They pause, observe, and respond in a thoughtful manner. They recognize the emotional needs of others and adjust their communication style accordingly. Developing emotional intelligence takes practice. It starts with self-awareness, followed by empathy, patience, and a commitment to respectful dialogue.

Communication is not only about words. It is about tone, timing, intention, emotion, understanding. While misunderstandings, conflicts, and breakdowns are part of every workplace, they do not have to harm relationships or productivity if handled well. By listening actively, managing emotions, being culturally aware, and striving for clarity, professionals can handle even the most difficult communication situations with grace and confidence. Building strong communication habits leads to more cooperation, fewer conflicts, and a more respectful work culture.

Remember, great communication is not just about speaking. It is about connecting, repairing, and understanding beyond words.

****

# CHAPTER – III : GLOBAL AND CROSS-CULTURAL COMMUNICATION

*Bridging Differences Across Global Cultures*

## *Part-1: Across Borders and Minds: Understanding Cross-Cultural Communication and Its Pitfalls*

In today's globalized world, communication often transcends borders. With the rise of international business, travel, and digital technology, individuals frequently find themselves interacting with people from diverse cultural backgrounds. This has made cross-cultural communication an essential skill for personal and professional growth.

However, communicating across cultures is not without its challenges. What is considered polite, respectful, or effective in one culture may not hold the same meaning in another. Misunderstandings, misinterpretations, and conflicts are common when people from different cultures interact, especially if they do not understand the cultural context of each other's communication styles.

This chapter delves into the importance of cross-cultural communication, the common pitfalls, and practical strategies to navigate these challenges. By understanding the complexities of communicating across cultures, individuals can build stronger, more respectful relationships and become better global citizens.

**The meaning of Cross-Cultural Communication:** Cross-cultural communication refers to the process of exchanging ideas, information, and messages between people from different cultural backgrounds. It involves both verbal and non-verbal communication and is influenced by cultural norms, values, and beliefs. These cultural factors shape how people express themselves, interpret others' messages, and respond to different situations.

For instance, in some cultures, direct communication is valued, while in others, indirect communication is preferred to avoid confrontation. Understanding these cultural differences is crucial for effective communication.

Cross-cultural communication is not limited to international business or travel. In multicultural societies, people from different cultural backgrounds interact on a daily basis in workplaces, schools, and communities. Misunderstandings in such settings can lead to frustration, confusion, and even conflict.

**Role of Culture in Communication:** Culture plays a significant role in shaping how people communicate. It influences language, behavior, attitudes, and the way emotions are expressed. A culture is like a lens through which individuals view the world, and it affects how they convey and interpret messages.

One of the primary cultural differences in communication is the distinction between high-context and low-context cultures. High-context cultures rely heavily on implicit communication, where much of the message is conveyed through context, non-verbal cues, and shared understanding. In contrast, low-context cultures value direct communication, where the meaning of the message is conveyed explicitly in words.

Understanding the difference between high-context and low-context cultures is essential to avoid misunderstandings. For example, if a person from a low-context culture speaks directly to someone from a high-context culture, the message might be perceived as harsh or impolite.

**Non-Verbal Communication and Its Importance:** Non-verbal communication is just as important, if not more so, than verbal communication in cross-cultural interactions. Non-verbal cues such as facial expressions, body language, gestures, posture, eye contact, and tone of voice can carry significant meaning.

However, the interpretation of these non-verbal cues varies greatly across cultures. For example, a firm handshake is considered a sign of confidence and respect in many Western cultures, while in some Asian cultures, a softer handshake may be preferred. Similarly, direct eye contact may be seen as a sign of attentiveness and trustworthiness in some cultures, but in others, it might be interpreted as rude or confrontational.

In addition to gestures and eye contact, other non-verbal cues like personal space can vary from culture to culture. In some cultures, people are comfortable standing close to one another when speaking, while in others, maintaining more physical distance is important. Misreading non-verbal cues can lead to serious misunderstandings and conflicts. Therefore, it is important to develop an awareness of how non-verbal communication differs across cultures and to pay close attention to these cues during interactions.

**Common Pitfalls in the Cross-Cultural Communication:** While cross-cultural communication can be enriching, there are several pitfalls that individuals need to avoid. These pitfalls can arise due to differing cultural norms, values, and communication styles.

One of the most significant challenges in cross-cultural communication is making assumptions based on stereotypes. Stereotyping involves making broad generalizations about a group of people based on limited information, often ignoring the diversity within that group. For example, assuming that all people from a certain country or region behave the same way or share the same values is not only inaccurate but also disrespectful.

Stereotypes can lead to misunderstandings, hurt feelings, and even reinforce negative biases. To avoid this pitfall, it is important to approach each individual as a unique person and not judge them solely based on their cultural background.

Language barriers are another common challenge in cross-cultural communication. Even if both parties speak a common language, such as English, differences in vocabulary, idioms, accents, and pronunciation can lead to confusion. Certain words or phrases that are widely understood in one culture may be meaningless or offensive in another.

For instance, the word "pants" in American English refers to trousers, but in British English, it can mean underwear. Such differences in language can cause misunderstandings and awkward situations. It is essential to be mindful of language differences and take extra care to ensure clarity when speaking with someone from a different linguistic background.

Context is a crucial factor in understanding communication. As mentioned earlier, cultures differ in the way they use context to convey meaning. A statement that may seem innocent or neutral in one culture could carry a different or even negative connotation in another.

For example, in some cultures, it is important to ask indirect questions and give responses that are context-sensitive rather than direct. Ignoring the cultural context can lead to misinterpretation, as someone may say one thing but mean another.

To avoid such misunderstandings, it is vital to ask questions for clarification and to be patient when trying to interpret someone's words and actions. Adapting to the context of the conversation can improve the quality of communication.

Silence in communication can have different meanings in different cultures. In some cultures, silence is seen as a sign of respect and thoughtfulness, while in others, it may be perceived as discomfort or reluctance to engage.

For example, in many Asian cultures, silence is often used to show respect or to give others time to think before responding. In contrast, in many Western cultures, silence can be uncomfortable and might lead people to think that the conversation has ended or that there is a problem.

Understanding the role of silence in communication helps prevent misunderstandings. It is important to be aware of how silence is perceived and to adjust your expectations accordingly when interacting with people from different cultural backgrounds.

**Strategies for Effective Cross-Cultural Communication:** While cross-cultural communication can be challenging, there are several strategies that individuals can adopt to improve their interactions and avoid common pitfalls.

The first step in effective cross-cultural communication is developing cultural awareness. This involves learning about the cultural norms, values, and communication styles of the people you interact with. This knowledge helps in avoiding misunderstandings and adjusting your communication approach accordingly.

You can develop cultural awareness by reading books, attending cultural training programs, and engaging with people from different cultures. Understanding the context of their communication will give you the tools to interact more effectively.

When in doubt, ask questions. If you are unsure about something someone has said, do not be afraid to seek clarification. Asking open-ended questions can help you gain a better understanding of the other person's perspective and ensure that you are both on the same page.

It is important to ask questions respectfully and with an open mind. Rather than making assumptions or jumping to conclusions, clarifying the meaning behind someone's words can prevent miscommunication.

Cross-cultural communication requires flexibility and the willingness to adapt. You may need to adjust your communication style to suit the person you are speaking with. This could involve modifying your tone, pace of speech, or non-verbal cues.

Being open-minded means not only accepting but also appreciating cultural differences. Embrace diversity and learn from it. It will enrich your communication skills and help you build stronger, more meaningful relationships across cultures.

Respect is a universal value, but it is expressed differently across cultures. In all cross-cultural interactions, it is essential to show respect for the other person's values, beliefs, and communication style. This can be done by listening actively, being patient, and acknowledging the other person's perspective. Treating others with respect builds trust and creates a positive environment for effective communication.

Cross-cultural communication is an essential skill in the modern world. As the global workforce becomes more interconnected, understanding and navigating cultural differences is more important than ever. Misunderstandings and communication breakdowns are inevitable, but they can be mitigated with the right knowledge, mindset, and strategies.

By developing cultural awareness, being mindful of language and non-verbal cues, and adopting an open-minded and respectful approach, individuals can overcome the pitfalls of cross-cultural communication. In doing so, they can build stronger relationships, foster collaboration, and thrive in diverse environments.

In the end, effective cross-cultural communication is about recognizing that while we may come from different backgrounds, we all share the same desire to be understood and respected. By embracing our differences and communicating thoughtfully, we can create a more connected, empathetic world.

***Section Closed...***

## *Part-2: Empathy in Action: How Empathy and Sympathy Shape Human-Centric Communication*

Communication is one of the most essential aspects of human interaction. Whether we are in a personal relationship, a professional environment, or simply conversing with strangers, the way we communicate can make all the difference in fostering understanding and connection. Among the many elements that influence communication, empathy and sympathy are two of the most powerful forces. They shape how we relate to one another, providing the emotional depth needed for meaningful interactions. Although often used interchangeably, empathy and sympathy serve distinct roles in human communication. Understanding the difference between them and how each contributes to communication is key to improving both our personal relationships and professional interactions.

**Empathy vs. Sympathy: The Basics**: Empathy and sympathy are both emotional responses that play vital roles in human interactions, but they differ significantly in their nature and effect. Empathy is the ability to understand and share the feelings of another person. It goes beyond simply recognizing that someone is feeling a particular way – it involves putting oneself in the other person's shoes and feeling what they are feeling. This emotional connection helps build trust, understanding, and stronger relationships.

Sympathy, on the other hand, involves acknowledging another person's suffering or difficult situation and feeling concern or sorrow for them. Unlike empathy, which requires emotional engagement, sympathy does not demand that you fully experience the other person’s emotions. Instead, it is about feeling compassion or pity for them from a somewhat external perspective. Sympathy is typically more detached than empathy, and while it expresses care and concern, it does not always lead to the same level of connection.

Both empathy and sympathy are important, but they serve different purposes in communication. Empathy allows us to connect on a deeper emotional level, while sympathy offers comfort and reassurance, often when emotional engagement is not appropriate or needed.

**The Power of Empathy in Communication**: Empathy is one of the most powerful tools in communication. It goes beyond words, creating an emotional bond between individuals. It enables us to understand not only what someone is saying but also how they are feeling and why they feel that way. This deeper understanding fosters respect and trust, which are crucial components of any healthy relationship.

In personal relationships, empathy allows us to connect with others on a profound level. When we empathize with someone, we are able to share in their joy, sadness, frustration, or excitement. This shared experience helps create a sense of belonging and reinforces the emotional connection between people. By demonstrating empathy, we communicate to others that we are not just listening to their words, but that we truly understand their emotional state.

Empathy is also a crucial component of active listening. In active listening, we focus not only on what the other person is saying but also on their non-verbal cues, such as body language, tone of voice, and facial expressions. These cues often reveal a deeper layer of meaning that words alone cannot convey. An empathetic listener is attuned to these cues and responds in a way that shows they understand not only the content of the conversation but also the emotions behind it.

In professional environments, empathy has a significant impact on workplace dynamics. Leaders who demonstrate empathy are more effective in motivating their teams, building trust, and resolving conflicts. When employees feel that their managers understand their concerns, they are more likely to be engaged and motivated in their work. Empathy also plays a key role in conflict resolution, as it allows individuals to understand the underlying emotions behind disagreements and find solutions that respect everyone's feelings. In customer service, empathy can greatly improve the customer experience. When service representatives empathize with customers, they can offer more personalized solutions and address concerns in a way that feels genuinely caring. This emotional connection can transform a negative experience into a positive one, resulting in greater customer loyalty and satisfaction.

**Empathy and Active Listening**: Active listening is an essential skill that goes hand in hand with empathy. It involves fully concentrating on the speaker, understanding their message, and responding thoughtfully. Active listening requires more than just hearing the words; it demands paying attention to the speaker's tone, body language, and emotions. Empathy takes this a step further, allowing us to truly feel what the other person is feeling.

When we actively listen with empathy, we are not only absorbing information but also showing the speaker that their emotions and thoughts matter. This kind of engagement can help to diffuse tense situations, resolve conflicts, and strengthen relationships. Empathetic listening involves showing the other person that we are present in the moment with them, that we understand their perspective, and that we care about how they feel.

An example of empathetic listening might occur in a workplace setting when an employee is expressing frustration with a project.

Rather than simply offering advice or solutions right away, an empathetic listener would take the time to understand why the employee feels frustrated, acknowledge their emotions, and then offer support or suggestions that align with their feelings.

**Sympathy in Communication**: While empathy requires deep emotional engagement, sympathy tends to be more detached. Sympathy involves recognizing another person's distress and feeling pity or sorrow for their situation, but without fully engaging in their emotional experience. Though it lacks the depth of empathy, sympathy still plays an important role in communication.

Sympathy can be particularly helpful when someone is going through a difficult time, such as dealing with loss or a personal setback. Offering sympathy in these situations allows us to express our concern and provide comfort, even if we do not fully understand or experience the pain the other person is feeling. Sympathy can act as a supportive gesture, acknowledging the person's suffering and letting them know that they are not alone.

However, sympathy has its limitations. Because it involves a certain level of emotional distance, it may not always be as effective as empathy in creating deep connections. While sympathy can be comforting, it does not foster the same sense of shared understanding that empathy does. In some cases, sympathy may even create a barrier between people, as it can make the person offering sympathy seem distant or disconnected from the situation.

In professional settings, sympathy can be useful in situations where emotional engagement is not necessary. For instance, offering sympathy to a colleague who has experienced a personal loss can show that you care, even though you may not fully understand what they are going through. Sympathy in these situations allows for an appropriate, respectful response without necessarily becoming emotionally involved.

**The Balance Between Empathy and Sympathy:** The key to effective communication lies in knowing when to employ empathy and when to use sympathy. Both are valuable, but they should be used in the right context. Empathy is ideal for situations where a deeper emotional connection is needed. It is especially valuable when addressing personal concerns, offering support, or resolving conflicts. Empathy creates trust and strengthens relationships by allowing people to feel understood and validated.

On the other hand, sympathy can be appropriate when we want to express care and concern but do not need to fully engage in the other person's emotional experience. Sympathy can be useful in situations where deep emotional involvement is unnecessary or when the other person may need space to process their feelings independently.

In professional environments, both empathy and sympathy have their place. Empathy can help foster a positive work culture, build trust, and resolve conflicts, while sympathy can provide comfort during difficult times. Striking the right balance between empathy and sympathy can help individuals navigate complex emotional landscapes and communicate in a way that is both caring and effective.

Empathy and sympathy are both essential components of human communication. While empathy involves deeply understanding and sharing in the emotions of others, sympathy offers a more detached, yet compassionate, response. Both play important roles in how we connect with others, both in personal relationships and in professional settings.

Empathy allows us to build deeper, more meaningful connections with others. It fosters trust, improves active listening, and enhances emotional intelligence. Sympathy, though less intimate, still plays a crucial role in providing comfort and expressing care, especially in situations where emotional distance is necessary. By understanding and applying empathy and sympathy in our communication, we can foster more compassionate, human-centric interactions that enhance both personal and professional relationships.

Ultimately, the ability to balance empathy and sympathy can transform how we communicate, creating an environment where people feel truly understood, supported, and valued. Whether in times of joy, sorrow, frustration, or conflict, empathy and sympathy provide the emotional foundation needed for meaningful and effective communication.

***Section Closed...***

## *Part-3: Diverse Voices, One Team: Inclusive Communication in Multicultural Environments*

In today's globalized world, the ability to communicate effectively in multicultural environments is more important than ever. As teams and organizations become more diverse, understanding how to engage in inclusive communication has become essential for fostering collaboration, productivity, and mutual respect. Multicultural environments bring together people from different backgrounds, each with their own unique perspectives, beliefs, and values. For these environments to thrive, it is crucial to ensure that communication is inclusive, respectful, and fosters understanding. This chapter will explore the significance of inclusive communication, the challenges faced in multicultural environments, and strategies to improve communication and ensure that every voice is heard and valued.

**An Inclusive Communication**: Inclusive communication goes beyond just the words spoken; it encompasses the entire process of interaction between individuals from diverse backgrounds. At its core, inclusive communication ensures that everyone feels respected, understood, and valued, regardless of their cultural, linguistic, or personal differences. This practice is crucial in both personal and professional settings, where effective communication is key to achieving common goals.

Inclusive communication fosters an environment where people feel safe to express themselves. When individuals believe their perspectives and contributions are valued, they are more likely to participate actively, share ideas, and engage with the team. This sense of belonging enhances morale and leads to higher levels of creativity, innovation, and problem-solving.

In professional environments, inclusive communication helps in building strong, cohesive teams. When people from different backgrounds are able to communicate openly and respectfully, it creates a collaborative atmosphere where all team members feel empowered to contribute. This is particularly important in multicultural workspaces, where diversity can be a significant asset if managed well.

**Understanding Cultural Diversity in Communication**: Cultural diversity is the presence of people from different cultural backgrounds within a group or society. Culture affects communication in numerous ways, including language, non-verbal cues, and social norms. When working in multicultural environments, it is important to recognize and understand the various cultural differences that may influence how people communicate.

Language is one of the most apparent cultural differences that impact communication. In a multicultural setting, people may speak different languages, dialects, or have varying levels of proficiency in the common language of the workplace. This can lead to misunderstandings, misinterpretations, communication barriers. In such environments, it is important to use clear and simple language, avoid jargon, and be patient with those who may not be fluent in the language being spoken.

Non-verbal communication is another area where cultural differences can affect communication. For example, in some cultures, maintaining direct eye contact is seen as a sign of respect, while in others, it may be considered rude or aggressive. Similarly, gestures, body language, and personal space can vary greatly between cultures. Being aware of these differences can help individuals avoid unintentional offenses and ensure that their messages are received as intended.

In addition to language and non-verbal cues, social norms and values play a significant role in communication. For instance, in some cultures, people may be more inclined to speak indirectly to avoid conflict, while others may prefer to be more direct and assertive. Understanding these cultural nuances can help individuals navigate potential conflicts and communicate more effectively with people from diverse backgrounds.

**Facing Challenges in Multicultural Communication**: While multicultural environments offer many opportunities for growth and innovation, they also present a range of challenges. One of the primary challenges is the potential for miscommunication. Differences in language, cultural norms, and communication styles can lead to misunderstandings, confusion, and frustration. Without a clear understanding of these differences, people may unintentionally offend others or fail to convey their intended message.

Another challenge is unconscious bias. Unconscious biases are the automatic assumptions and stereotypes that people make about others based on their background, appearance, or other characteristics. These biases can influence how individuals perceive and communicate with others, leading to inequality and exclusion. For example, someone from a minority group may feel overlooked or dismissed because of unconscious bias, which can affect their ability to contribute effectively to the team.

Power dynamics also play a significant role in multicultural communication. In some cultures, there is a strong emphasis on hierarchy and respect for authority, while in others, equality and open dialogue are prioritized. These differences can lead to communication barriers, as people from hierarchical cultures may be reluctant to speak up or challenge authority, while those from egalitarian cultures may struggle to understand this reluctance.

Finally, cultural differences in the way people express emotions can lead to misunderstandings. Some cultures may place a strong emphasis on emotional restraint, while others may encourage open displays of emotion. This difference in emotional expression can create tension or lead to misinterpretation of intentions and feelings.

**The Role of Active Listening in Inclusive Communication**: Active listening is a key component of inclusive communication. It involves not only hearing the words spoken but also paying attention to the speaker's emotions, body language, and non-verbal cues. In multicultural environments, active listening becomes even more critical, as it ensures that individuals feel heard and understood, regardless of their cultural background.

One of the key aspects of active listening is giving the speaker your full attention. This means not interrupting, making eye contact, and being present in the moment. In multicultural environments, it is important to be patient and allow people to express themselves fully, especially if they are speaking in a second language or using a communication style that may be different from your own.

Another important aspect of active listening is showing empathy. Empathy involves understanding and sharing the feelings of the speaker. In multicultural environments, empathy helps bridge the gap between different cultural perspectives and demonstrates that you are making an effort to understand the other person's point of view. This emotional connection can create a sense of trust and foster a more inclusive communication environment.

In addition to active listening, it is essential to ask clarifying questions when necessary. In multicultural environments, misunderstandings can arise due to differences in language or cultural norms. Asking questions to ensure that you fully understand the speaker's message can prevent confusion and help facilitate more effective communication.

**Building an Inclusive Communication Culture:** Building an inclusive communication culture requires effort from everyone involved, from leadership to team members. It starts with fostering an environment where people feel comfortable expressing themselves without fear of judgment or exclusion. Leaders play a crucial role in setting the tone for inclusive communication by modeling respectful and open dialogue.

One way to promote inclusive communication is by encouraging diversity in the workplace. This includes not only hiring people from diverse backgrounds but also ensuring that everyone has an equal opportunity to contribute. Diversity should be celebrated, and individuals should feel that their unique perspectives are valued.

Training and education also play a vital role in building an inclusive communication culture. Workshops and seminars on cultural awareness, unconscious bias, and effective communication can help individuals understand the challenges of multicultural communication and develop the skills needed to navigate them. Providing language training or resources to improve language proficiency can also help ensure that everyone has the tools they need to communicate effectively.

Another important aspect of building an inclusive communication culture is creating spaces where people can share their experiences and ideas. This can be achieved through team meetings, brainstorming sessions, and informal discussions. By creating these opportunities for open dialogue, organizations can foster a culture of mutual respect and understanding, where everyone feels empowered to share their thoughts and opinions.

**Overcoming Communication Barriers**: In multicultural environments, communication barriers are inevitable, but they are not insurmountable. One of the first steps in overcoming these barriers is recognizing that they exist. Acknowledging that people come from different cultural backgrounds with different communication styles is the first step in fostering understanding.

To overcome language barriers, organizations can invest in language training and resources such as translation services or language assistance tools. Encouraging employees to be patient and open-minded when dealing with language differences can also help alleviate frustration and promote effective communication.

Another important step in overcoming communication barriers is addressing unconscious bias. Organizations can take steps to reduce bias by providing training on cultural competence, challenging stereotypes, and promoting diversity and inclusion initiatives. By fostering an environment that values diversity and inclusivity, organizations can help mitigate the impact of unconscious bias on communication.

Inclusive communication in multicultural environments is essential for building strong, effective teams and fostering a culture of mutual respect and understanding. By recognizing and addressing the challenges posed by cultural differences, language barriers, and unconscious bias, organizations can create environments where every voice is heard and valued. Active listening, empathy, and an openness to diverse perspectives are key components of inclusive communication that can help bridge cultural gaps and promote collaboration.

Ultimately, embracing inclusive communication not only benefits individuals within the organization but also contributes to the overall success of the team or organization. By cultivating an environment where diverse voices are respected and included, organizations can unlock the full potential of their teams and create a more harmonious, productive, and innovative work environment.

****

# CHAPTER - IV : COMMUNICATION FOR GROWTH AND SUCCESS

*Skills That Shape Personal Progress*

## *Part-1: Student Speak: Communication Skills Every Learner Should Master*

Communication is the backbone of success in every field. For students, mastering communication skills is not just about acing exams or finishing assignments. It is about making meaningful connections with peers, teachers, and professionals that pave the way for academic, personal, and future career success. Clear, effective communication fosters understanding, reduces conflicts, and opens doors for new opportunities. Whether it's written, verbal, or non-verbal, communication is an integral part of a student's growth journey.

For any student navigating the challenges of learning, developing robust communication skills is paramount. The goal is not only to convey information but to do so in a manner that is understood and appreciated by others. This chapter delves into the essential communication skills that every student must master, offering insights on how these skills contribute to academic success and life beyond school.

**Why Communication Skills Matter for the Student**: Effective communication is the key to educational achievement. From explaining complex ideas in class to participating in group discussions, the ability to communicate plays a huge role in how students engage with the academic world. It's not just about talking or writing; it's about ensuring that the message is clear, coherent, and convincing. Good communication makes students stand out among their peers and helps them gain respect from their teachers and classmates.

Additionally, communication skills extend beyond the classroom. Whether students are applying for jobs, attending interviews, or collaborating with colleagues in their future workplaces, strong communication is a valuable asset. The world is increasingly interconnected, and students who master the art of communication are better equipped to succeed in the global marketplace. Communication skills enable students to build relationships, resolve conflicts, and share their ideas in a way that influences others positively.

**Verbal Communication**: Verbal communication is perhaps the most fundamental skill students need. It involves the ability to speak clearly and coherently in various settings, including classroom presentations, group discussions, and casual conversations. Mastering verbal communication is not only about being able to talk but also about ensuring that one's ideas are understood by others. One of the primary components of effective verbal communication is clarity. Students must learn how to express their thoughts in a simple, clear, and direct manner. Avoiding unnecessary jargon or overly complicated language is crucial in making sure the listener understands the message without confusion. Additionally, students should work on their vocabulary and grammar, as this adds credibility to their spoken words.

Another important aspect is the tone of voice. The tone can significantly impact the message being conveyed. A warm, friendly tone makes the speaker seem approachable and engaging, while a harsh or monotone voice can make even the best ideas seem uninviting. Being mindful of one's tone helps create a positive atmosphere during conversations and presentations.

**Listening Skills**: Effective communication doesn't only involve speaking but also listening. Listening is an often-overlooked aspect of communication that holds equal importance. Without good listening skills, communication breaks down. Students must learn to actively listen to what others are saying. Active listening requires full attention to the speaker, understanding the message, and providing feedback or responses that show comprehension.

Active listening is essential in classroom discussions, group projects, and one-on-one conversations with teachers and peers. It encourages an exchange of ideas where all parties feel heard and understood. Students who are good listeners are able to engage more deeply in discussions, ask relevant questions, and contribute thoughtfully to group conversations.

**Non-Verbal Communication**: Non-verbal communication refers to the body language, facial expressions, gestures, posture, and other physical cues that convey meaning without words. It plays a critical role in how students communicate with others, as non-verbal cues can sometimes express more than what is said verbally.

For example, body posture can indicate whether a student is engaged, relaxed, or disinterested. Eye contact demonstrates attentiveness and respect, while avoiding eye contact can be interpreted as discomfort or evasiveness. A smile or frown can express feelings or emotions that words may not fully capture.

When it comes to non-verbal communication, students should be aware of their body language and how it might be perceived by others. Being conscious of these signals can help students project confidence, warmth, and professionalism. Likewise, understanding the non-verbal cues of others allows students to gauge how their messages are being received, which is important for effective communication.

**Written Communication**: Writing is another critical aspect of communication that students must master. Whether writing essays, reports, emails, or even social media posts, being able to express ideas in writing clearly and concisely is an essential skill. Good written communication requires students to be precise in their choice of words, organized in their ideas, and mindful of grammar and spelling.

Students must learn how to structure their writing properly, making sure that each paragraph connects logically to the next. This ensures that the ideas flow smoothly and are easy to follow. A well-written piece should have an introduction that sets the context, a body that elaborates on the main ideas, and a conclusion that wraps up the discussion.

The clarity of the message is also paramount in written communication. Ambiguity or vagueness in writing can confuse readers, and students should aim to be as specific as possible. Additionally, students should pay close attention to tone. A professional, respectful tone is essential in academic writing and correspondence with teachers. On the other hand, more casual tones can be used in personal communication with friends or peers, but students should still strive to remain clear and respectful.

**Public Speaking**: Public speaking is a key skill that students should master, especially as they prepare to enter the professional world. Whether giving a class presentation or speaking at a school event, being able to speak confidently in front of an audience is invaluable. Public speaking is often a source of anxiety for many students, but with the right preparation, anyone can become a confident speaker.

Students should begin by preparing their content well in advance. Thorough research, organizing the content logically, and practicing the delivery are essential steps in ensuring a successful presentation. Rehearsing in front of a mirror, recording oneself, or even presenting to a friend or family member can help students build confidence in their speaking ability.

Beyond content, students should focus on their delivery. Speaking slowly and clearly allows the audience to follow along. Students should avoid rushing through their speech, as this can lead to missed points and confusion. Additionally, using appropriate gestures and maintaining eye contact with the audience helps to engage them and makes the presentation feel more interactive.

**Interpersonal Communication:** Interpersonal communication involves the exchange of information, feelings, and ideas between individuals. It is crucial for students in both personal and academic contexts. Whether working on group projects or participating in extracurricular activities, students must learn how to engage with others effectively.

One key component of interpersonal communication is empathy. Empathy involves understanding and sharing the feelings of another person. When students practice empathy, they build stronger, more meaningful relationships with their peers. It also allows them to navigate difficult conversations and conflicts with sensitivity and understanding.

Another essential interpersonal skill is conflict resolution. In any social setting, disagreements are bound to arise. Students should learn how to address conflicts in a constructive manner. Instead of getting defensive or angry, they should focus on listening to the other person's perspective and working together to find a solution. Practicing conflict resolution helps students maintain positive relationships with others and promotes a healthy, collaborative environment.

**Communication in Digital Spaces**: In today's digital age, much of the communication students engage in takes place online. From sending emails to participating in online class discussions and social media interactions, students must learn how to communicate effectively in digital spaces.

One key aspect of online communication is clarity. In the absence of non-verbal cues such as body language and facial expressions, it is especially important for students to be clear and concise in their written messages. Students should avoid using excessive abbreviations or informal language that could lead to misunderstandings.

**Feedback and Constructive Criticism**: Receiving and giving feedback is an integral part of communication that students must master. Feedback, whether positive or constructive, helps students improve their skills, enhance their performance, and grow both personally and professionally.

Students should learn how to accept feedback gracefully, without becoming defensive or discouraged. They should view feedback as an opportunity for growth and use it to improve their work. Additionally, students must also learn how to provide constructive feedback to others. Offering feedback in a respectful, supportive manner helps create a learning environment that encourages continuous improvement.

Mastering communication skills is a lifelong process that can have a profound impact on a student's academic and personal life. By becoming proficient in verbal and non-verbal communication, writing, public speaking, and interpersonal interactions, students equip themselves with the tools they need to succeed. Communication is not only about transmitting information but also about connecting with others and creating meaningful, positive interactions.

For students, the ability to express ideas clearly, engage in meaningful discussions, and collaborate effectively with others will be invaluable throughout their lives. As they continue to refine these skills, they become more confident communicators, capable of navigating a wide range of social and professional settings with ease. The foundation of strong communication begins early in a student's journey and provides them with the skills to achieve success in their educational and professional endeavors.

***Section Closed...***

## *Part-2: The Working Communicator: Speaking, Writing, and Leading with Influence in Your Career*

In the modern workplace, communication is not merely a skill; it is the essence of professional success. The ability to convey ideas clearly and persuasively is a crucial component in achieving career goals. Whether you are speaking in meetings, writing emails, or leading teams, communication is at the heart of every professional interaction. The working communicator knows that the way they express themselves, both in speech and writing, plays a significant role in how they are perceived and how effectively they can influence others.

Mastering the art of communication involves developing skills that allow you to be clear, confident, and influential in all forms of communication. It is not just about being able to speak or write; it is about doing so with purpose, clarity, and impact. This book is designed to help you understand how communication shapes your career and provide practical strategies for improving your speaking, writing, and leadership abilities.

**The Power of Effective Speaking**: Public speaking is a powerful tool for any professional. Whether presenting to a group of colleagues, addressing a client, or speaking at a conference, the ability to speak with clarity and confidence can set you apart from others in your field. Speaking effectively is not just about delivering information—it's about engaging your audience, creating rapport, and making a lasting impression.

Effective speaking starts with preparation. Before you speak, whether it's a formal presentation or an informal meeting, it's essential to know your audience and the message you want to convey. Understanding your audience allows you to tailor your language and tone to resonate with them. When preparing a speech or presentation, structure is crucial. A clear introduction, body, and conclusion will help your audience follow your ideas with ease.

While preparing is key, delivery is equally important. The way you speak can influence how your message is received. Speaking clearly, at a measured pace, and with a confident tone will ensure that your message is not only heard but understood. Additionally, body language plays a huge role in effective speaking. Maintaining eye contact, using gestures, and adopting an open posture will make you appear more approachable and engaged.

For many professionals, public speaking can be intimidating. However, with practice, confidence grows. One way to build confidence is through rehearsal. Practicing your speech in front of a mirror or with a trusted colleague can help you refine your delivery. If you are giving a presentation, it can also help to use visual aids such as slides or charts to support your message and keep the audience engaged.

**Writing with Clarity and Purpose**: In the professional world, written communication as important as spoken communication. From emails and reports to proposals and memos, writing is the primary means of sharing information, instructions, and ideas in the workplace. However, not all writing is equally effective. Writing with clarity, purpose, and conciseness is vital to ensuring that your message is understood and acted upon.

One of the first steps to writing effectively is understanding your purpose. Are you informing, persuading, or requesting? Once you have a clear purpose, it will be easier to structure your writing in a way that achieves your goal. For instance, if you are writing an email to request something, begin with a direct and polite request, followed by the necessary details. In contrast, a report might need an introduction that outlines the purpose, a body that elaborates on the details, and a conclusion that summarizes key points and action steps.

Concise writing is also a hallmark of effective communication. In the professional world, time is valuable, and long-winded emails or reports can quickly become overwhelming. Being brief does not mean sacrificing important details; it means focusing on what's necessary and avoiding superfluous information. Each sentence should contribute to the overall message, and redundancy should be eliminated.

Moreover, the tone of your writing plays a crucial role in how your message is received. Professional writing should maintain a respectful and polite tone, even when delivering bad news or expressing disagreement. It's essential to be mindful of your language and avoid overly casual or harsh tones, as these can create misunderstandings or conflict.

Proofreading is another essential element of effective writing. Errors in grammar, spelling, or punctuation can detract from your message and hurt your professional image. Always take the time to review your work before sending it out, and use tools such as grammar checkers to help you spot mistakes.

**The Power of Leadership and Communication**: Leadership and communication are inextricably linked. A leader's ability to communicate effectively can influence team morale, productivity, and success. Leaders must be able to convey their vision, set expectations, motivate their team, and address issues—all while maintaining clear and open communication.

One of the key aspects of leadership communication is the ability to inspire. Great leaders know how to articulate a compelling vision and motivate others to join them in achieving that vision. This requires passion, clarity, and the ability to connect emotionally with others. The language a leader uses must be both inspiring and accessible. Using motivational language can help inspire confidence in your team and encourage them to work toward a common goal.

Equally important is the ability to listen. Leadership is not just about talking; it's also about listening to your team's concerns, ideas, and feedback. Effective leaders create an environment where team members feel heard and valued. This fosters trust and collaboration, leading to a more productive and engaged team. Leaders should actively listen to their team members, ask questions, and show empathy for their concerns. By doing so, they create an open dialogue that fosters innovation and problem-solving.

Clear communication is also critical for managing expectations. Leaders must clearly define roles, responsibilities, and goals to ensure that everyone on the team understands what is expected of them. Regular communication about progress, feedback, and adjustments keeps everyone aligned and helps prevent misunderstandings.

**Role of Influence in Communication**: Influence is a central element of communication in any career. Whether you are negotiating a deal, trying to persuade a client, or leading a team, the ability to influence others is invaluable. Influence is not about manipulation; it is about guiding others toward a decision or action that aligns with shared goals or values.

Effective communicators are skilled at persuading others through logical arguments, emotional appeal, and credibility. One of the most effective tools for persuasion is storytelling. By framing your message within a narrative, you can make your argument more relatable and memorable. Stories evoke emotions and can help your audience see the practical implications of your ideas.

Building credibility is also essential for influence. When people trust you and believe in your expertise, they are more likely to be influenced by your ideas. Consistency in your words and actions helps build trust over time. Being honest, transparent, and ethical in your communication strengthens your credibility and increases your influence.

Moreover, knowing your audience is a key aspect of influencing others. Tailoring your message to the needs, values, and perspectives of your audience increases the likelihood that your communication will have the desired effect. Whether you are speaking to a colleague, a client, a large audience, understanding what motivates them will help you craft a message that resonates.

**The Importance of Adaptability in Communication**: In the workplace, communication is not one-size-fits-all. Different situations and people require different approaches. Being able to adapt your communication style to the context and audience is a vital skill for career success. A good communicator can switch between formal and informal tones, adjust their language for different audiences, and be flexible in their approach to delivering information.

For example, when communicating with senior executives or clients, you may need to use formal language, emphasize strategic goals, and present data-driven arguments. In contrast, when speaking with peers or subordinates, a more informal, conversational tone might be more effective. Adapting to the communication style of others is also important. Some people prefer direct, to-the-point communication, while others may appreciate a more collaborative, discussion-based approach.

Flexibility in communication is also crucial when dealing with conflict. In tense situations, a calm and measured approach can help defuse emotions and facilitate resolution. Adapting your communication style to the situation at hand shows emotional intelligence and allows you to navigate challenges effectively.

In today's competitive professional environment, communication is an essential skill for career advancement. Whether you are speaking in meetings, writing reports, or leading teams, the way you communicate can make or break your success. Being an effective communicator requires practice, self-awareness, and adaptability. By focusing on clarity, confidence, and empathy, you can improve your speaking, writing, and leadership abilities, leading to greater influence in your career.

Mastering these communication skills will not only help you achieve your professional goals but will also build stronger relationships, enhance your reputation, and position you as a leader in your field. In the workplace, communication is not just a skill—it is the pathway to success. By becoming a better communicator, you can unlock countless opportunities for growth and advancement in your career.

***Section Closed...***

## *Part-3: Speak to Get Hired: Winning Interviews, Building Resumes, and Creating Lasting Impressions*

In today's competitive job market, securing a job requires more than just technical expertise or qualifications. How you communicate plays a significant role in determining your success during the hiring process. From the initial stages of crafting a resume to the final interview, communication skills are vital. The ability to clearly articulate your skills, showcase your qualifications, and leave a lasting impression on potential employers can be the difference between being hired and being overlooked.

This book explores the key aspects of communication that every job seeker must master. It provides insights into how to prepare for interviews, how to write a compelling resume, and how to create a strong impression that will help you land the job. Whether you are just beginning your job search or are looking to enhance your communication strategies, this guide offers valuable techniques that can boost your chances of success.

**Winning Interviews**: Interviews are a crucial part of the hiring process. They provide employers with the opportunity to assess a candidate's suitability for the role, while also allowing candidates to demonstrate why they are the right fit for the company. How you present yourself during an interview can significantly impact your chances of getting hired.

Preparation is key to acing your interview. Before the interview, take time to research the company, understand its culture, and review the job description. Being knowledgeable about the company's mission and values shows that you are genuinely interested and have put effort into learning more about the organization.

You should also anticipate common interview questions and practice your responses. Some questions, such as "Tell me about yourself," "What are your strengths and weaknesses?" or "Why do you want to work here?" are likely to come up in almost every interview. By preparing answers to these questions ahead of time, you can respond confidently and avoid feeling flustered. Practice in front of a mirror or with a friend to refine your answers and improve your delivery.

**Remember this when you are attending an interview:** Imagine you're sitting in an interview, and the interviewer asks you, "Why do you want to work here?" Now, a textbook answer might be something like, "I believe in your company's mission, and I think my skills align with the role." It sounds polished, but it lacks that real connection that can make a difference.

Instead, if I were answering this question with a more down-to-earth approach, I might say something like, "To be honest, what drew me here is the kind of work you're doing. I've seen how your team approaches challenges, and that's the kind of environment I thrive in. I've always been someone who likes to tackle problems head-on, but.I also like learning from others in a team setting. Your company seems like a place where I can really grow, contribute, and see tangible results from my efforts, and that's something that excites me."

Notice how this answer is more genuine; it's not just following a script, but instead, it's expressing an honest reason for wanting to be there, while also demonstrating self-awareness about how you fit into the company culture. It feels real because it touches on personal motivations and aligns with the actual environment you're aiming for. It's not about giving the "right" answer; it's about communicating what really resonates with you and how you see yourself contributing.

Now, let's say you're asked, "Tell me about a time when you faced a challenge at work." Instead of launching into a rehearsed example from a book of interview tricks, a real-world response might look something like this: "I remember once when we had a major project with tight deadlines, and there were a lot of moving parts. It seemed like no matter what we did, something was always falling behind. We had to reassess our priorities multiple times. I realized that instead of pushing harder, we needed to step back, take a deep breath, and focus on communicating more effectively within the team. It wasn't a quick fix, but by being transparent and addressing concerns openly, we managed to stay on track and deliver the project on time. What I learned from that was how crucial clear communication and collaboration are, especially in high-pressure situations."

What's different about this response is that it's not just a clean-cut story with all the right buzzwords. It's reflective, it shows vulnerability, and it shares a learning experience. It's clear that you're thinking critically about the situation, and you're speaking from a place of experience rather than just regurgitating an answer from a guidebook. This type of response gives the interviewer a better sense of who you are as a person, how you think, and how you approach problems in real life.

In interviews, especially when you're asked to share personal experiences or challenges, there's often a temptation to fall into the trap of sounding too perfect or rehearsed. The key here is to show authenticity. If there were a mistake made or a lesson learned, don't be afraid to admit it, because that's what makes your answer human. You're not just giving an answer that checks off all the boxes, you're offering insight into how you handle situations, think on your feet, and reflect on your actions.

The interviewer will likely appreciate the honesty and depth in your answers, and they'll get a clearer picture of how you might handle situations at work. That kind of transparency and self-awareness is much more relatable than delivering a scripted answer that sounds too polished to be true.

Let's also think about how these plays into something like feedback. When you're asked about how you handle feedback, many people would go for a perfect response like, "I welcome feedback because I see it as a way to improve." While that's nice, it can feel a bit impersonal or rehearsed. A real-world approach might sound like, "I've always valued feedback, but early on, I didn't always know how to handle it well. Sometimes it felt tough to hear, but I came to realize that the more I listen and reflect, the more it helps me grow in the long run. I try to approach feedback with a mindset of improvement, whether it's praise or constructive criticism, because ultimately, it's an opportunity to get better at what I do."

This type of answer shows that you're not just going through the motions; you're giving a thoughtful, reflective answer based on your real growth process. It's not about saying what you think they want to hear; it's about expressing your genuine thoughts on feedback and showing your evolution over time.

In an interview setting, it's easy to focus too much on giving the "right" answer, especially when you're nervous or trying to impress. But what really stands out is when you can speak from a place of sincerity, reflect on your experiences, and show your thought process.

Being genuine and transparent in your responses can help you connect with the interviewer on a human level, which is often what they're looking for. They're not just interested in whether you know the textbook answer; they're more interested in who you are as a person, how you think, and how you will fit into the team.

So, when you're answering interview questions, try to resist the urge to simply provide the expected answers. Instead, think about what feels real to you, what you've learned, and how you can convey that honestly. The more authentic you can be, the more your answers will resonate with the interviewer, and ultimately, they will give you a better sense of whether this is the right fit for you—and whether you're the right fit for them.

Interviews are a two-way street. While you're trying to present yourself in the best light possible, you're also trying to gauge whether the company and role are a good match for you. So it's important to speak authentically, even if it feels a bit uncomfortable at times. If you're being honest and true to yourself, you'll not only perform better, but you'll also get a clearer sense of whether the role and environment align with your goals, values, and personality.

Effective communication during the interview is just as important as your qualifications. Employers are not only assessing your technical skills but also evaluating your personality, attitude, and communication style. Speak clearly and with confidence. One of the most important aspects of communication is clarity. Speak slowly and clearly, avoiding filler words such as "um," "uh," or "like." Pausing before answering a question can give you time to collect your thoughts and respond in a more organized manner. Speaking with confidence helps to convey that you believe in your abilities and are sure of your qualifications.

Maintaining eye contact and using positive body language plays a significant role in how your message is received. Make sure to maintain eye contact with the interviewer to convey trustworthiness and engagement. Additionally, use open body language, avoid crossing your arms, and smile. Positive body language helps establish rapport and makes you appear approachable and confident.

Listening is a critical skill in communication. During the interview, listen carefully to the interviewer's questions and respond thoughtfully. Active listening demonstrates that you are engaged and respectful of the interviewer's perspective. Don't interrupt while the interviewer is speaking, and wait until they have finished before responding.

Interviews often have a limited time frame, so it's important to stay focused on the question being asked and provide concise responses. Avoid rambling or going off on tangents. The goal is to answer the question fully without providing unnecessary details. Use the STAR method (Situation, Task, Action, Result) to structure your answers, particularly when addressing behavioural questions.

Enthusiasm is also key. Employers are more likely to hire candidates who show genuine interest in the position. When responding to questions, convey excitement and enthusiasm for the job. This can be achieved by highlighting what excites you about the opportunity and explaining how your skills and experiences align with the company's needs.

**Building a Strong Resume**: Your resume is your first opportunity to showcase your skills, qualifications, and experiences. A well-crafted resume can open doors to interviews, while a poorly written one may result in your application being overlooked.

Start by ensuring your resume is tailored to the job you're applying for. Highlight the skills and experiences that are most relevant to the position. A generic resume is less likely to catch the employer's attention, while a targeted one demonstrates your focus and attention to detail. Customize your resume for each job application by incorporating the keywords from the job description and emphasizing the skills the employer is seeking.

The layout and design of your resume are equally important. It should be clean, professional, and easy to read. Use a simple font, such as Arial or Calibri, and avoid cluttering the document with unnecessary graphics or complex formatting. Hiring managers often review resumes quickly, so it's essential to make sure your resume is easy to skim and highlights the most important information.

Begin with a clear and concise summary or objective statement at the top of your resume. This should briefly explain who you are, what you bring to the table, and what you are seeking in your next role. Follow this with your professional experience, listing your most recent job first and working backward. For each position, include a list of your key responsibilities and accomplishments, making sure to quantify your achievements where possible.

Education should be listed after your work experience, especially if you are more experienced. Include your degrees, certifications, and relevant coursework. If you have completed any industry-specific training, such as workshops or certifications, be sure to include these as well.

If applicable, include a section for relevant skills, such as technical proficiencies, language abilities, or specialized knowledge that may be valuable to the position.

Finally, make sure to proofread your resume for spelling, grammar, and formatting errors. A resume filled with mistakes sends the message that you lack attention to detail. Consider having a friend or mentor review it before submitting your application.

**Creating Lasting Impressions:** Once the interview is over, your communication skills should not stop. Creating a lasting impression involves the steps you take after the interview to reinforce your qualifications and interest in the position.

One of the most effective ways to create a lasting impression is by sending a thoughtful thank-you note or email. This should be done within 24 hours of the interview. In the note, express your gratitude for the opportunity to interview, reiterate your interest in the position, and highlight a key point or two from the interview that reaffirm your fit for the role. A well-written thank-you note shows professionalism and reinforces your enthusiasm for the job.

Follow up with a polite inquiry about the timeline for the hiring process if you haven't heard back after the expected timeframe. Lastly, the way you handle rejection can also leave a lasting impression. If you are not selected for the position, ask for feedback on your interview performance. Thank the interviewer for their time and express your interest in future opportunities with the company.

Mastering the art of interviewing, crafting a compelling resume, and creating a lasting impression are all essential components of the job search process. By preparing for your interview, clearly communicating your skills, and following up thoughtfully, you can greatly increase your chances of securing the job. Effective communication doesn't stop after the interview—it's an ongoing process that can make a significant difference in your career. By honing these skills, you'll not only be more successful in interviews but also more confident in your ability to connect with potential employers and colleagues.

****

# CHAPTER – V : THE POWER OF SPEAKING, READING, LISTENING AND WRITING (LSRW)

*Mastering All Four Communication Skills*

## *Part-1: Speaking Skills Development: Enhancing Verbal Communication for Effective Interaction*

In today's fast-paced world, the ability to communicate effectively is more important than ever. Whether you're in a casual conversation, a formal business meeting, or delivering a public speech, the way you speak can leave a lasting impact on your audience. Strong speaking skills are fundamental to building relationships, fostering collaboration, and creating positive impressions in both professional and personal settings. The ability to communicate clearly and persuasively can significantly influence your success in various areas of life. This section delves into the critical components of speaking skills development, offering practical insights into how you can improve your verbal communication for more effective interaction.

**Understanding the Importance of Verbal Communication**: Verbal communication is one of the primary ways we express our thoughts, ideas, and feelings. Whether you are speaking with a colleague, a friend, or a larger audience, how you communicate can shape how you are perceived, how your message is received, and whether your conversation leads to desired outcomes. Effective communication requires a combination of both verbal and non-verbal cues. While body language, facial expressions, and tone of voice play a significant role, the words we use and how we structure our speech are the foundation of clear and meaningful interaction.

Speaking skills development, therefore, is not just about mastering pronunciation or learning new vocabulary. It involves understanding how to deliver a message in a way that is engaging, clear, and appropriate for the context. It is about adapting your communication style based on the audience and ensuring that your words resonate and convey the intended meaning.

**Clarity and Precision in Speech**: One of the first and most crucial elements of effective speaking is clarity. Speaking clearly ensures that your message is understood and that the listener does not have to strain to figure out what you are trying to say. Whether you are having a one-on-one conversation or addressing a group, clarity can significantly impact how your message is received.

To speak clearly, it is essential to enunciate your words properly. Poor articulation can make it difficult for your audience to follow along, even if the content of your message is strong. Practicing proper enunciation helps prevent misunderstandings and ensures that your audience can easily grasp the key points you are trying to convey.

Another important factor in clarity is volume. Speaking too softly can make it hard for people to hear you, especially in larger rooms or noisy environments. On the other hand, speaking too loudly can come across as overbearing or aggressive. It is important to adjust your volume based on the setting and the size of your audience. Finding the right balance will ensure that your speech is audible without being overwhelming.

**Confidence in Speaking**: Confidence is an essential aspect of effective speaking. When you speak with confidence, it enhances your credibility and makes your message more persuasive. People are more likely to listen to and trust someone who expresses themselves with confidence. On the other hand, speaking nervously or with uncertainty can lead to doubt in your words and message.

Building confidence in speaking can be achieved through practice. The more you practice, the more comfortable you become with speaking in various situations. Whether you are rehearsing for a presentation or practicing in front of a mirror, gaining familiarity with the material you are presenting will help you feel more in control of your words.

Another way to build confidence is by focusing on your strengths. Rather than concentrating on potential mistakes or shortcomings, focus on your ability to deliver valuable information. This shift in mindset helps build self-assurance, making you more comfortable with the idea of speaking in front of others.

**Tone and Emotion in Communication**: Tone of voice is a powerful tool in verbal communication. It not only helps convey meaning but also communicates emotions, intentions, and attitudes. The way you say something often carries more weight than what you actually say. A positive, warm tone can make your message more engaging, while a cold or monotone tone can leave your audience disengaged.

When delivering your message, it is important to ensure that your tone aligns with the content. For example, if you are delivering exciting news, a lively and upbeat tone can amplify the message and make it more impactful. In contrast, if you are discussing a serious topic, a calm and steady tone is more appropriate. The ability to vary your tone based on the emotional content of your message adds depth and richness to your communication.

The tone also plays a role in conveying your level of sincerity. A heartfelt message delivered with genuine emotion can build trust and strengthen relationships. On the other hand, a message that sounds disingenuous or flat may cause the listener to question your sincerity.

**Pace and Timing of Speech**: The speed at which you speak also influences how your message is received. Speaking too quickly can overwhelm your audience and make it difficult for them to keep up with your points. Conversely, speaking too slowly may cause your audience to lose interest or find the conversation tedious.

Finding the right pace is crucial to maintaining the attention of your listeners. Adjusting your speed based on the context of the conversation allows you to emphasize key points and create a natural flow in the dialogue. For instance, when presenting important information, speaking more slowly and deliberately can help the audience absorb the material. In casual conversations, a moderate pace may feel more natural and comfortable.

It is also essential to pause at appropriate moments. Pausing after making a significant point allows your audience to reflect and absorb the information. Additionally, pauses can be used to add dramatic effect or emphasize key ideas. A well-timed pause can create suspense, allowing you to engage your listeners even more deeply.

**Active Listening and Responsiveness**: Effective communication is not just about speaking well but also about listening actively. Active listening involves being fully present in the conversation, paying attention to the speaker, and responding thoughtfully. By listening attentively, you are better able to tailor your response to the specific needs of the conversation, which can lead to more meaningful interactions.

When you actively listen, you show that you value the other person's perspective and are genuinely interested in what they have to say. This builds trust and strengthens relationships. In a conversation, you can demonstrate active listening by asking relevant follow-up questions, acknowledging key points, and offering thoughtful feedback.

Active listening is especially important in professional settings. It enables you to understand your colleagues' ideas and concerns and helps foster a collaborative work environment. It also helps you better respond to clients, understand their needs, and provide solutions that align with their goals.

**Body Language and Non-Verbal Communication**: Non-verbal communication plays a significant role in how your spoken words are received. Your body language, facial expressions, gestures, and eye contact all provide additional context to your message. For instance, maintaining eye contact while speaking conveys confidence and sincerity, while crossing your arms can signal defensiveness or discomfort.

In addition to reinforcing your spoken words, body language can also serve as a tool for managing how others perceive you. Good posture, open gestures, and an engaged demeanor can make you appear more approachable and trustworthy. On the other hand, closed-off body language, such as avoiding eye contact or slouching, can make you appear disengaged or disinterested.

It is essential to ensure that your body language is consistent with your verbal message. If your words convey one message while your body language communicates something different, it can lead to confusion or mixed signals.

**Overcoming Communication Barriers**: Throughout your life, you may encounter various communication barriers that hinder effective interaction. These barriers can include physical distractions, language differences, cultural misunderstandings, emotional biases, or even technological issues. Recognizing these barriers is the first step in overcoming them.

If you are speaking with someone who speaks a different language, for example, it is important to use simple, clear language to ensure understanding. You may also consider using visual aids or gestures to help clarify your message. In cross-cultural communication, being aware of different norms and customs can help you avoid misunderstandings and ensure that your message is received in the intended way.

Similarly, when dealing with emotional barriers, such as stress or frustration, it is important to remain calm and composed in your speech. Being aware of your emotions and how they influence your tone and body language can help you communicate more effectively, even in challenging situations.

**Public Speaking and Presentations**: Public speaking is an essential skill that many people find intimidating. However, it is a skill that can be developed with practice and preparation. When speaking in front of an audience, your goal is to engage and connect with them. You want your words to resonate and leave a lasting impact.

Effective public speaking involves careful preparation, practice, and delivery. It is essential to know your material inside out and to be able to present it in a structured and coherent manner. The more familiar you are with the content, the more confident and natural you will sound.

Delivery is equally important. A good speaker varies their tone, pace, and body language to maintain the audience's attention. They also engage the audience by making eye contact, asking questions, and encouraging participation.

Speaking is one of the most valuable skills you can develop in both your personal and professional life. Whether you are speaking to a colleague, presenting to a large audience, or engaging in casual conversation, your ability to communicate effectively plays a significant role in how your message is received and understood. By focusing on clarity, confidence, tone, pace, active listening, and non-verbal communication, you can enhance your speaking skills and improve your ability to interact with others.

Effective speaking is not something that happens overnight. It requires practice, self-awareness, and a commitment to continuous improvement. By dedicating yourself to refining your speaking skills, you will be better equipped to express yourself clearly, build stronger relationships, and succeed in various aspects of life.

***Section Closed...***

## *Part-2: Listening Skills Enhancement: Improving Active Listening and Comprehension Abilities*

Effective communication involves much more than speaking. One of the most vital aspects of communication, often overlooked, is listening. Listening, particularly active listening, is not just about hearing words; it is about fully understanding and processing the message being communicated. Active listening plays a key role in personal and professional relationships, helping to avoid misunderstandings, fostering empathy, and ensuring that messages are received as intended.

Listening is often perceived as a passive activity, where a person simply absorbs information without actively engaging. However, active listening is an intentional process that requires concentration, focus, and an understanding of both verbal and non-verbal cues. Enhancing listening skills can greatly improve how we interact with others, solve problems, and make informed decisions. In this chapter, we will explore the importance of listening, the different types of listening, and practical strategies for enhancing listening skills.

**The Importance of Active Listening**: The importance of active listening cannot be overstated. In both personal and professional settings, it helps build strong relationships, prevent conflicts, and ensure effective communication. For example, in a workplace setting, active listening fosters collaboration and teamwork. When team members actively listen to one another, they are better able to understand different perspectives and work together more effectively. In personal relationships, active listening helps individuals feel heard and validated, strengthening bonds and trust.

Active listening also plays a crucial role in reducing misunderstandings. When people are not actively engaged in listening, they are more likely to misinterpret or ignore important details. This can lead to confusion, frustration, and missed opportunities. By practicing active listening, individuals can ensure that they fully understand the speaker's message and respond appropriately.

**Barriers to Effective Listening**: There are several barriers to effective listening that can hinder communication. These barriers can be internal or external and can arise from various factors. Recognizing and addressing these barriers is essential for improving listening skills and enhancing comprehension.

One of the most common barriers to effective listening is external distractions. Noises, interruptions, and multitasking can all make it difficult to focus on the speaker. For instance, trying to listen to someone while checking your phone or working on a computer can cause your attention to shift, resulting in missed information.

Another barrier to effective listening is the tendency to form judgments or assumptions before fully hearing the speaker’s message. If the listener is quick to judge or is already set in their opinions, they may dismiss what is being said without truly understanding the speaker’s point of view. Prejudices and assumptions can cloud judgment and prevent the listener from considering new perspectives.

Strong emotions, such as anger, frustration, or excitement, can also interfere with listening. When people are emotionally charged, they may be too focused on their own feelings to absorb the message being communicated. In such situations, the listener may miss key details or misinterpret the speaker’s intentions.

Sometimes, listeners may not be interested in the topic being discussed. Lack of interest can lead to disengagement, making it difficult for the listener to retain or process the information being shared. When someone is not interested, they may stop paying attention, leading to misunderstandings or a failure to respond appropriately.

Physical barriers, such as hearing difficulties or fatigue, can also impact listening abilities. When individuals have difficulty hearing or are exhausted, it becomes harder for them to concentrate on the speaker. These barriers can be addressed by using assistive devices, taking breaks to avoid fatigue, or seeking a quieter environment to improve focus.

**Types of Listening**: There are several types of listening, each serving a different purpose in communication. Understanding the different types of listening can help individuals develop the skills needed to be effective listeners in various situations.

Active listening is the most engaged form of listening. It requires the listener to give their full attention to the speaker and to respond thoughtfully. Active listening involves not only hearing the words but also understanding the underlying emotions and intentions behind the message. This type of listening promotes a deeper level of communication, as the listener is actively engaged in the conversation and can provide thoughtful feedback.

Reflective listening is a similar form of listening where the listener reflects on what the speaker has said by paraphrasing or summarizing the message. This helps the speaker feel heard and provides an opportunity for clarification if needed. Reflective listening is often used in counseling, conflict resolution, and situations where emotions are involved.

Empathetic listening goes beyond understanding the message. It involves feeling what the speaker is feeling, putting yourself in their shoes, and offering support and understanding. Empathetic listening is crucial in personal relationships and situations where emotional support is needed.

Critical listening involves analyzing and evaluating the message. It requires the listener to think critically about the information being presented, considering its validity, relevance, and impact. Critical listening is often used in professional and academic settings, where decision-making and problem-solving are important.

**Improving Active Listening Skills**: Improving active listening skills is essential for anyone who wants to become a more effective communicator. The first step in improving listening skills is to eliminate distractions. This includes turning off electronic devices, finding a quiet space, and focusing entirely on the speaker. By doing so, the listener can give their full attention to the message and ensure that nothing important is missed.

The second step is to practice mindfulness. Mindfulness involves being present in the moment and focusing on the speaker's words, tone, and body language. By being mindful, listeners can pick up on both verbal and non-verbal cues, improving their overall understanding of the message.

Asking clarifying questions is another important technique for improving listening. If the listener does not fully understand something, they should ask questions to gain more clarity. This shows the speaker that the listener is engaged and interested in understanding their perspective.

Another key technique is to avoid interrupting the speaker. Interrupting can disrupt the flow of conversation and prevent the listener from fully absorbing the message. Instead, the listener should allow the speaker to finish their thoughts before responding. This shows respect for the speaker and ensures that the message is received accurately.

**The Role of Non-Verbal Cues in Listening**: Non-verbal cues, such as facial expressions, body language, and eye contact, play a significant role in communication. These cues can provide additional context and meaning to the spoken words. For example, a person who is speaking with a smile or open posture may be conveying warmth and friendliness, while someone who is crossing their arms or avoiding eye contact may appear defensive or disinterested.

By paying attention to non-verbal cues, listeners can gain a better understanding of the speaker's emotions and intentions. This is especially important in sensitive conversations, where emotions may not be explicitly stated but are conveyed through body language and tone of voice.

**The Benefits of Active Listening in Personal and Professional Life**: Active listening is a valuable skill that can improve both personal and professional relationships. In the workplace, active listening can lead to better teamwork, fewer misunderstandings, and improved problem-solving. When team members actively listen to each other, they are more likely to collaborate effectively and generate creative solutions. Active listening also helps to build trust and respect between colleagues, leading to a more positive work environment.

In personal relationships, active listening strengthens bonds and fosters empathy. When people feel heard and understood, they are more likely to open up and communicate more effectively. Active listening also helps to resolve conflicts by ensuring that both parties fully understand each other's perspectives and emotions.

In conclusion, active listening is a vital skill that plays a crucial role in effective communication. By overcoming barriers to listening, understanding the different types of listening, and implementing techniques for improvement, individuals can enhance their listening abilities and become more effective communicators. Active listening fosters better relationships, reduces misunderstandings, and helps individuals make more informed decisions. Whether in personal or professional settings, active listening is an essential tool for building strong connections and ensuring clear, meaningful communication.

***Section Closed...***

## *Part-3: Reading Skills Mastery: Developing Speed and Comprehension for Effective Reading*

Reading is one of the most vital skills for personal and professional development. In today's fast-paced world, effective reading goes beyond merely decoding words; it involves understanding, analyzing, and retaining information. Whether you're reading for leisure, education, or professional purposes, being able to read efficiently and comprehend effectively can significantly impact how much knowledge you absorb and how well you apply that knowledge.

Reading is not just a skill; it's a tool that shapes the way we think, process information, and communicate with others. Strong reading skills can make a significant difference in how quickly and deeply we understand various subjects, and how we navigate different scenarios that require mental agility and fast learning.

To improve reading skills, two essential components must be focused on: reading speed and comprehension. Both of these are vital to ensure that you not only read quickly but also understand the material well enough to apply it. In this chapter, we will explore the importance of reading skills, delve into the elements that contribute to reading speed and comprehension, and provide strategies to enhance these skills for better results.

**The Importance of Reading Skills**: Reading is foundational to almost every activity we engage in daily. From emails to books, articles, and instructions, the ability to read efficiently is essential in almost every aspect of life. Strong reading skills help us grasp complex concepts, stay informed, and access information more effectively, all of which contribute to personal and professional growth.

Effective reading goes hand in hand with effective learning. To acquire knowledge, whether for a career, a hobby, or personal growth, you need the skill to process and understand what you're reading. Poor reading skills can create barriers to learning, while strong reading skills open doors to a wealth of information. Reading allows you to learn new concepts, enhance your vocabulary, and become more versatile in your thinking. It also helps you retain information, allowing you to apply what you've read in real-world scenarios.

Reading is not just a passive activity; it is a dynamic process that involves engaging with the text, analyzing the content, and synthesizing information to form a deeper understanding. It enables critical thinking, problem-solving, and better decision-making, all of which are invaluable skills in any profession. Strong reading skills also make it easier to stay informed, broaden your horizons, and maintain curiosity throughout life.

**Speed and Comprehension: The Key Components of Effective Reading**: Effective reading is a balance between speed and comprehension. Speed refers to how quickly you can read the text, while comprehension involves how well you understand the material. While many people focus on one or the other, the true power of reading comes from improving both aspects simultaneously.

The goal is to read faster without sacrificing understanding. This is especially important in professional and academic settings, where time is often limited, and the volume of material can be overwhelming. Being able to skim through information and extract the main points quickly is an essential skill that can improve productivity. However, it is just as important to ensure that you fully understand what you're reading and retain the key details.

In many cases, people assume that reading faster means sacrificing comprehension. While this is true to some extent, it doesn't have to be the case. With practice and the right strategies, you can enhance both your reading speed and your ability to comprehend the material.

**Developing Speed Reading Skills**: Speed reading is a technique used to increase reading speed without significantly compromising comprehension. While it is true that reading faster requires practice and skill, it is also important to understand that speed reading does not mean rushing through the text carelessly. Rather, it involves improving your ability to focus, minimize distractions, and use effective techniques to process information quickly.

One of the most effective techniques for speed reading is eliminating subvocalization. Subvocalization is the habit of silently pronouncing each word in your head as you read. While this may seem natural, it significantly slows down your reading pace. Instead, try to reduce the tendency to "hear" the words in your mind and focus on reading groups of words instead. This technique, called chunking, allows you to process several words at once, which speeds up your reading without losing comprehension.

Another strategy to improve reading speed is using your peripheral vision. Rather than focusing on individual words, try to expand your gaze to take in whole phrases or even entire sentences at a time. The more you train your eyes to take in multiple words simultaneously, the faster you will read.

It's also beneficial to preview the material before you dive into reading. Skim through headings, subheadings, and any bold or italicized text. This will give you an overview of the content and help you focus on the most important parts. Skimming before reading helps you orient yourself to the material, making it easier to read quickly and absorb the essential points.

Finally, practice makes perfect. Speed reading is a skill that improves with time. The more you practice, the more natural it will become, and the quicker you will be able to process information while maintaining a strong level of comprehension.

**Understanding Comprehension**: While reading speed is important, comprehension is just as crucial. Comprehension refers to your ability to understand, interpret, and retain the material you are reading. If you are reading quickly but not fully grasping the content, then the time spent reading is not productive. To improve comprehension, it is essential to actively engage with the text rather than passively gliding through the words.

Active reading is an essential strategy for improving comprehension. It involves interacting with the text by asking questions, making predictions, and reflecting on what you are reading. Instead of just reading the words, engage with the content. Think about the key points, the arguments being presented, and the overall structure of the material. Actively questioning the material and drawing connections between ideas helps deepen your understanding.

Another important technique is rereading. Sometimes, the first time you read a passage, it may not be clear. Going over the text a second or third time can often provide clarity and deepen your understanding. After rereading, summarize the main points to ensure that you've understood the material correctly.

One of the most powerful ways to enhance comprehension is to make connections between what you read and your existing knowledge. Relating new information to concepts you already understand makes the material easier to process and remember. For example, when reading a book or article, think about how the new information aligns with or challenges your current knowledge. This process of making connections helps reinforce your learning and aids retention.

**Retention: Remembering What You Read**: Reading is not just about understanding the material; it's also about remembering it. Retention allows you to recall and apply the knowledge you've gained from your reading. Effective retention depends on how actively you engage with the content.

One technique that can help with retention is spaced repetition. Spaced repetition involves reviewing information at gradually increasing intervals over time. Studies have shown that this technique helps reinforce memories and ensures that information sticks. By periodically revisiting material, you can improve long-term retention and make it easier to recall key details when you need them.

Another method for improving retention is summarizing. After reading, take a few minutes to write a summary of what you've learned in your own words. This helps solidify the information in your mind and makes it easier to recall later. Summarizing also helps you identify the key takeaways from a text and reinforces the main ideas.

Creating mental images of the content can also aid retention. Visualizing the material as you read makes it more memorable. When you read about a particular concept, try to form a mental picture of it. This process helps your brain store the information in a way that is easier to recall later.

**Adapting Reading Strategies for Different Types of Content**: Different types of reading materials require different strategies. For instance, when reading fiction, your goal is usually to understand the plot, characters, and themes. Reading fiction is often more relaxed, and comprehension is the primary focus rather than speed.

Non-fiction texts, on the other hand, often require a more analytical approach. When reading for academic or professional purposes, your focus is typically on extracting key points, analyzing arguments, and understanding concepts. In these cases, skimming for essential information and taking notes can help you process the material more efficiently.

For professional reading, efficiency is key. When reading emails, reports, or articles, try to focus on key facts and essential details. Skimming and scanning are often effective for this purpose, allowing you to extract the relevant information without getting bogged down by unnecessary details.

In conclusion, mastering reading skills is essential for personal and professional development. By focusing on speed, comprehension, and retention, you can enhance your ability to process and understand the vast amounts of information that we encounter daily. Through practice and by applying the right strategies, you can become a more effective reader, absorbing knowledge more efficiently and retaining it for longer periods. Whether for leisure, education, or work, reading remains one of the most valuable skills you can develop.

***Section Closed...***

## *Part-4: Writing Skills Mastery: Improving Clarity, Coherence, and Creativity in Writing*

Writing is a powerful tool for communication, and developing strong writing skills can significantly enhance your ability to express yourself and connect with others. Whether you're crafting an email, a report, a novel, or a research paper, your ability to write clearly, coherently, and creatively can set you apart. Writing is more than just putting words together on a page; it involves structuring your thoughts, organizing your ideas, and presenting them in a way that is both engaging and easily understood. Mastering writing skills is essential for anyone who wants to communicate effectively, whether professionally or personally.

The art of writing requires attention to detail, understanding of language, and the ability to convey ideas in a manner that resonates with readers. Good writing is not just about grammar and spelling; it's about the ability to make your ideas clear, connect them logically, and infuse creativity into the process. As you work to develop these skills, you'll find that your writing becomes a more powerful tool for expression and influence.

In this chapter, we will explore the importance of writing skills, focusing on three critical aspects: clarity, coherence, and creativity. These elements are the backbone of strong writing, and mastering them will improve your ability to communicate more effectively in any context. By honing these skills, you can take your writing from basic to exceptional, making a lasting impact on your readers.

**The Importance of Clarity in Writing**: Clarity is the foundation of good writing. If your writing is unclear, your message will get lost, no matter how insightful or valuable the content may be. Writing with clarity means expressing your ideas in a straightforward and understandable manner, ensuring that your readers can easily grasp the points you're trying to make. Without clarity, even the most interesting ideas can be muddled, confusing, or misinterpreted.

To write clearly, it's essential to focus on sentence structure. Simple and direct sentences are easier to follow than long, convoluted ones. Avoid unnecessary complexity and jargon. Overcomplicating your writing can make it harder for your audience to engage with your message. Instead, strive for simplicity and precision. This doesn't mean you should limit yourself to basic vocabulary, but rather, choose words that are accessible to your audience and that express your ideas accurately.

One key aspect of clarity is avoiding ambiguity. When writing, make sure your sentences are specific and convey exactly what you mean. Vague statements or generalized language can leave your readers confused and unsure of your intent. For instance, instead of saying "the situation improved," specify how it improved and in what way. This added detail enhances clarity by providing a concrete image of what you're describing.

In addition to sentence structure and specificity, punctuation is also essential for clarity. Proper punctuation helps guide the reader through your writing and clarifies the meaning of sentences. For example, a misplaced comma can completely change the meaning of a sentence. Be mindful of punctuation rules and use them to enhance the clarity of your message. Regular practice and careful proofreading will help you develop a stronger understanding of punctuation and sentence structure.

**Creating Coherence in Your Writing**: While clarity is about making individual sentences easy to understand, coherence refers to how well your ideas flow together. A well-written piece is not just a collection of sentences; it's a connected series of thoughts that build upon one another to support the central message. Achieving coherence in writing means ensuring that your ideas are logically organized and that your writing progresses smoothly from one point to the next.

One effective way to achieve coherence is through proper organization. Start with an outline to map out the main ideas you want to cover. This will help you organize your thoughts and ensure that each section of your writing is connected to the next. A good structure, such as the introduction-body-conclusion format, can help provide a clear roadmap for your readers and guide them through your argument or narrative.

Each paragraph in your writing should have a clear main idea that relates to the overall topic. When writing essays, reports, or articles, each paragraph should support your central argument or contribute to the overall theme. Don't jump between unrelated ideas within a single paragraph. Instead, focus on one point at a time, and use transitions to connect paragraphs logically.

Transitions are words or phrases that help your writing flow more smoothly. They act as bridges between sentences and paragraphs, guiding your readers through your ideas. Common transition words include "however," "in addition," "for example," and "on the other hand." These words not only improve the flow of your writing but also help maintain coherence by showing relationships between different ideas.

Coherence is also enhanced by consistency in tone, voice, and style. Switching between formal and informal language or changing the tone without explanation can disrupt the flow of your writing and confuse the reader. By maintaining a consistent style throughout your work, you ensure that your message is clear and unified.

**The Role of Creativity in Writing**: While clarity and coherence are critical to good writing, creativity is what makes your work stand out. Creativity allows you to present your ideas in new and exciting ways that engage the reader's imagination and evoke emotion. Creative writing is not confined to fictional works; even in business, academic, or professional writing, creativity can make your writing more compelling and memorable.

One way to incorporate creativity into your writing is by using vivid language. Descriptive language helps paint a picture in the reader's mind, making your writing more engaging and immersive. For instance, instead of saying "the sunset was beautiful," you could say, "the sunset painted the sky in shades of orange and pink, casting a warm glow over the horizon." This creates a stronger visual image and draws the reader into the scene.

Another way to enhance creativity is by experimenting with different writing techniques, such as metaphors, similes, and personification. These figurative language tools allow you to express ideas more creatively and add depth to your writing. For example, instead of writing "she was angry," you could write "her fury boiled over like a storm cloud ready to burst." This comparison gives the reader a clearer picture of the emotion and makes the writing more engaging.

Creativity in writing also involves the way you approach your topic. Don't be afraid to think outside the box and approach your subject from a unique perspective. Whether you're writing a report, an essay, or a story, finding a fresh angle can make your work more interesting and memorable. Challenge yourself to think differently about the subject matter and explore new ideas and concepts that others might not have considered.

**The Importance of Regular Practice**: Like any skill, writing improves with regular practice. The more you write, the more comfortable you become with expressing your ideas and the better your writing will become over time. Writing is a skill that evolves, and consistent practice is key to improvement. Whether you write daily, weekly, or whenever you have time, the important thing is to make writing a habit.

One way to make writing a regular habit is to set aside dedicated time each day to write. It doesn't matter what you write about, as long as you practice. You could keep a journal, write short stories, create essays, or even write emails or blog posts. The goal is to write consistently, allowing you to develop your writing style and improve your clarity, coherence, and creativity.

In addition to regular writing practice, reading is also essential for improving your writing skills. Reading exposes you to different writing styles, vocabulary, and sentence structures that you can incorporate into your own work. By studying the works of skilled writers, you can learn valuable techniques and gain insight into how to write more effectively. Pay attention to how other writers organize their thoughts, use transitions, and develop their ideas. These observations can inform your own writing and help you refine your skills.

Mastering writing is a lifelong journey that requires patience, dedication, and a willingness to learn. Writing with clarity, coherence, and creativity is essential for effective communication. By focusing on these key elements, you can improve your ability to convey ideas clearly, connect your thoughts logically, and engage your readers with fresh and creative expressions.

Whether you're writing for academic purposes, professional communication, or personal expression, strong writing skills are invaluable. Writing is a powerful tool that can open doors, influence others, and help you achieve your goals. By practicing regularly, reading widely, and seeking feedback, you can continue to develop your writing skills and become a more effective communicator.

Remember that good writing is not about perfection; it's about progress. With each piece of writing, you learn something new and become a better writer. Embrace the process, be patient with yourself, and enjoy the journey of improving your writing skills.

****

# CHAPTER – VI : THE NOW AND NEXT

*Next Frontiers in Global Communication*

## *Part-1: The Intra-Personal Communication: Power, Purpose, and Possibility*

Intra-personal communication refers to the internal dialogue that occurs within an individual. This form of communication involves self-reflection, self-awareness, emotional regulation, and the constant processing of thoughts. Though often overlooked in favour of more visible forms of communication like interpersonal or group interactions, intra-personal communication forms the foundation of all external expressions. It is where intentions are shaped, decisions are made, and identities are built.

In today's rapidly evolving world, understanding the power of intra-personal communication is no longer optional. As the complexities of life increase, so does the need for individuals to engage in meaningful conversations with themselves. The present significance and the future potential of this internal dialogue are immense, impacting mental health, productivity, decision-making, and even the broader fabric of society.

**Understanding Intra-Personal Communication:** Intra-personal communication is the act of talking to oneself, whether aloud or silently. It includes conscious thought, unconscious mental processes, self-questioning, affirmations, and internalized beliefs. It can manifest as daydreaming, analyzing, rehearsing conversations, or even simple self-reflection. The quality of intra-personal communication influences how people perceive the world, respond to stimuli, and interpret experiences. It affects emotional intelligence, resilience, confidence, and ultimately, behavior. While the mind may appear silent to the outside world, it is often engaged in a constant stream of self-talk that can either uplift or hinder personal growth.

***Present Scope of Intra-Personal Communication:***

**(i) Mental Health and Emotional Balance:** One of the most significant areas where intra-personal communication is currently making an impact is mental health. As more people acknowledge the importance of mental well-being, there is a growing emphasis on the role of inner dialogue. Positive self-talk can reduce anxiety, increase motivation, and build emotional stability. Conversely, negative internal dialogue is often associated with depression, self-doubt, and anxiety disorders.

Therapies like Cognitive Behavioral Therapy (CBT) and Mindfulness-Based Stress Reduction (MBSR) focus heavily on helping individuals become aware of their thoughts. They encourage people to reshape their self-talk patterns, replacing damaging beliefs with constructive ones. This internal rewiring helps individuals gain control over their minds, making them less reactive and more intentional.

**(ii) Decision-Making and Problem Solving:** Every decision begins with an internal debate. From daily choices to life-altering decisions, intra-personal communication acts as the internal committee that weighs options, analyzes outcomes, and justifies actions. The better an individual is at understanding their values and processing information internally, the more effective they become at decision-making.

Individuals with strong intra-personal communication skills tend to make decisions that align with their core beliefs. They are less likely to be influenced by external pressure because they understand their internal compass. This clarity reduces regret, builds confidence, and sharpens critical thinking.

**(iii) Goal Setting and Motivation:** Self-motivation originates in one's internal dialogue. When individuals engage in encouraging self-talk, set intentions, and visualize outcomes, they create a roadmap for personal achievement. Intra-personal communication helps them set goals, stay focused, and track progress.

People who regularly check in with themselves through journaling, meditation, or self-reflection often display greater determination. They are able to analyze their failures, adjust their strategies, and celebrate their growth. Such individuals treat their inner voice not as a critic but as a coach, guiding them through challenges.

**(iv) Leadership and Personal Development:** In today's leadership training and personal development programs, intra-personal communication is becoming a key area of focus. Leaders who understand their own values, emotions, and thought processes are better equipped to lead others. They are more empathetic, decisive, and grounded.

Self-awareness, a core element of intra-personal communication, is considered a pillar of emotional intelligence. It enables individuals to recognize their triggers, regulate their emotions, and understand the impact of their behavior. As organizations shift toward inclusive and value-driven cultures, intra-personal development is seen as a competitive advantage.

**(v) Education and Learning:** In educational settings, intra-personal communication plays a crucial role in learning retention, comprehension, and creativity. Students who can reflect on what they have learned and apply it in new contexts are more likely to succeed academically. Metacognition, or thinking about thinking, is a skill that enhances memory and critical analysis.

Educators are now encouraging practices like reflective writing, learning journals, and personalized feedback. These strategies help students connect emotionally and intellectually with what they learn, making the knowledge more meaningful and memorable.

*Future Scope of Intra-Personal Communication*

**(i) Integration with Artificial Intelligence:** As artificial intelligence becomes a part of daily life, future applications may include tools that enhance intra-personal communication. From AI-powered journaling apps to virtual mentors that help with emotional reflection, technology could become a mirror for the inner self.

Such innovations may use biometric data, voice tone analysis, and behavioral tracking to offer insights into emotional states. They could prompt users to pause, reflect, or reframe their thoughts, serving as digital allies in personal growth. The fusion of intra-personal communication with AI may empower individuals to engage in more meaningful and productive internal dialogue.

**(ii) The Rise of Self-Coaching Models:** The future of personal development may see a shift from external coaching to self-coaching. This model relies heavily on intra-personal communication. As people gain access to structured frameworks and digital resources, they will be able to guide themselves through emotional and intellectual growth.

Self-coaching practices will include guided self-reflection, structured journaling, visualization, and internal dialogue simulations. These tools will help individuals navigate life transitions, career decisions, and personal challenges without always relying on external help.

**(iii) Mental Health Revolution:** The future of mental health care is likely to be proactive rather than reactive. Intra-personal communication will play a central role in this shift. Preventive mental health models will focus on equipping individuals with tools to recognize negative thought patterns before they escalate.

Mental health education in schools and workplaces will prioritize self-awareness, emotional regulation, and self-compassion. Mindfulness training, inner dialogue management, and personal reflection exercises will become standard practices. As stigma around mental health continues to fade, more people will openly engage in conversations with themselves as a means of healing and growth.

**(iv) Personal Branding and Identity Building:** In the digital age, personal branding is no longer restricted to celebrities or entrepreneurs. Everyone curates an identity, consciously or unconsciously. The ability to align one's public persona with one's true self requires robust intra-personal communication.

The future will demand authenticity, and those who engage deeply with their internal world will be best positioned to present a consistent and compelling identity. Whether for career advancement or social connection, understanding and expressing one's core beliefs, values, and emotions will become essential.

**(v) Global Citizenship and Empathy:** As the world becomes more interconnected, the need for global empathy will grow. Understanding others begins with understanding oneself. Intra-personal communication is the training ground for empathy and compassion.

Future leaders and changemakers will need to be deeply introspective to lead diverse teams, resolve conflicts, and advocate for social justice. Educational systems around the world will emphasize character education, self-reflection, and internal accountability to build responsible global citizens.

**Challenges and Misconceptions:** Despite its importance, intra-personal communication is often misunderstood. Many perceive self-talk as trivial or associate it with mental instability. Others may confuse it with overthinking, which is often unproductive and anxiety-inducing. There is also a lack of structured training on how to improve intra-personal communication. While public speaking and writing are taught, skills like reflection, self-inquiry, and emotional literacy are rarely included in formal curricula. This gap leaves many individuals unaware of the power and potential of their inner world. Another challenge is the prevalence of negative self-talk. Many individuals unknowingly engage in self-criticism, which erodes confidence and promotes fear. Breaking this cycle requires awareness and deliberate practice, which must be fostered through education and personal development.

**Cultivating an Intra-Personal Communication:** Developing strong intra-personal communication is a journey that requires patience and practice. It begins with becoming aware of the inner voice and understanding its tone, content, and triggers. Cultivating mindfulness helps individuals observe their thoughts without judgment.

Journaling is a powerful tool to externalize internal thoughts and gain clarity. It enables individuals to track patterns, identify limiting beliefs, and celebrate progress. Meditation and silence also allow space for internal dialogue to surface and be examined.

Affirmations and visualization exercises can gradually replace negative thought patterns with empowering beliefs. By consistently engaging in self-reflection and self-dialogue, individuals build resilience, confidence, and purpose. Intra-personal communication is the invisible thread that connects every aspect of human existence. It is the foundation of self-awareness, the engine of motivation, the compass of decision-making, and the sanctuary of emotional healing.

The present landscape already reflects a growing acknowledgment of its importance in mental health, education, leadership, and personal development. Looking ahead, intra-personal communication will become an indispensable life skill. It will be integrated into technology, mental health care, education systems, and leadership training. The future belongs to those who listen to themselves, understand themselves, and grow from within. In a world filled with noise, the ability to hear one's own voice will be the greatest superpower.

***Section Closed...***

### *Part-2: Mind the Gap: Bridging Generational Differences in Communication Styles*

Communication is at the core of human interaction, and its role cannot be overstated in any context, whether personal, educational, or professional. Effective communication allows individuals to understand each other, collaborate, and build relationships. In today's society, however, communication is becoming increasingly complex due to the presence of multiple generations interacting in shared spaces. In particular, the communication gap between generations can lead to misunderstandings, frustration, and missed opportunities for collaboration.

The Generational differences influence how individuals communicate, their expectations, and the ways in which they interact. With people from different generations working together, living in close proximity, or attending the same educational institutions, understanding these differences becomes essential for effective communication. This chapter explores how different generations communicate, the challenges these differences pose, and offers solutions to bridge the communication gap that often arises between Baby Boomers, Generation X, Millennials, and Generation Z.

The generations we are talking about, Baby Boomers, Generation X, Millennials, and Generation Z, each have their own unique communication style shaped by the societal, technological, and cultural influences they experienced during their formative years. Baby Boomers, born between 1946 and 1964, grew up in a time when face-to-face communication, formal language, and telephone calls were the primary modes of interaction. They often place a high value on direct communication, personal relationships, and respect for authority.

Generation X, born between 1965 and 1980, came of age during the rise of personal computers, fax machines, and the internet. They were exposed to both traditional and modern communication methods, making them more adaptable to technological advances. Generation X is typically comfortable with email, phone calls, and face-to-face meetings but may prefer more efficient and task-oriented communication. They value their independence and often view communication as a means to achieve specific outcomes rather than just a social exchange.

Millennials, born between 1981 and 1996, are digital natives, having grown up with the internet, cell phones, and social media. Their communication style tends to be fast-paced, informal, and often relies on text messaging, instant messaging, and social media platforms. Millennials appreciate quick responses and frequent feedback, using communication as a tool for both personal connection and professional networking. They tend to embrace more casual and flexible communication styles but can sometimes overlook formalities in professional settings.

Generation Z, born between 1997 and 2012, is the first generation to be fully immersed in the digital world from a young age. They communicate primarily through technology, using text messages, social media platforms, and video chats as their preferred methods. Generation Z tends to favor short, visual, and concise communication, often using emojis and gifs to express emotions and tone. While they may appear more informal, they value authenticity and directness in communication, seeking meaningful and transparent interactions.

The differences in communication styles between these generations can create tension, especially when they are required to work together or interact in professional environments. For example, a Baby Boomer manager may expect a formal email from an employee, while a Millennial may feel more comfortable using a casual, text-based communication style. Similarly, a Generation X employee may be frustrated by the perceived informality of a Generation Z team member's communication or find the reliance on instant messages unproductive.

Genrally, Communication challenges arise when generational communication preferences clash. For e.g., misunderstandings can occur when one generation misinterprets the tone of a message from another generation. What one group views as a straightforward, efficient way of communicating might be perceived as abrupt or rude by another. Additionally, the generational divide in technological fluency can create further friction. Older generations may feel left out of conversations that take place over social media or digital messaging platforms, while younger generations may struggle to engage with more traditional forms of communication, such as face-to-face meetings or formal reports.

These challenges are compounded by generational stereotypes. Baby Boomers may perceive younger generations as entitled or overly reliant on technology, while Millennials and Generation Z might view older generations as resistant to change or unable to keep up with technological advancements. These stereotypes can fuel frustration and hinder the development of effective communication strategies in both personal and professional contexts. Therefore, addressing the communication gap requires a multifaceted approach that fosters understanding, respect, and collaboration across generational lines.

One of the most important strategies to bridge the communication gap is promoting active listening. Active listening is the foundation of all good communication. It involves paying full attention to the speaker, understanding their message, and responding thoughtfully. Practicing active listening helps individuals from different generations to understand each other's perspectives and reduce misunderstandings. For instance, when a Baby Boomer listens actively to a Millennial or Generation Z colleague's communication, they may better appreciate the preference for brevity and informality in the message, rather than interpreting it as disrespectful or dismissive.

Active listening also encourages empathy, which is essential when dealing with generational differences. By understanding the reasons behind different communication styles, individuals can respond with greater sensitivity and avoid jumping to conclusions based on their own biases. Empathy fosters mutual respect and makes it easier for people from different generations to connect and communicate effectively.

Another strategy is flexibility and adaptability in communication. It is essential that individuals learn to adapt their communication styles based on the preferences of others. While it may be comfortable for a Baby Boomer to conduct a face-to-face meeting, they should be open to using technology when interacting with Millennials and Generation Z, who may prefer virtual meetings or email. Similarly, younger generations should make an effort to adapt to the more formal communication styles of older generations, especially in professional settings. Flexibility allows everyone to feel heard and respected, creating a more inclusive environment.

Leveraging the strengths of each generation can also help bridge the communication gap. Each generation has unique skills and qualities that contribute to the overall communication dynamic. Baby Boomers bring valuable experience, interpersonal skills, and a deep understanding of traditional communication methods. Generation X offers a practical, no-nonsense approach to communication and is highly skilled in using both traditional and digital tools. Millennials are creative and highly adept at using digital platforms to facilitate communication, while Generation Z brings a fresh perspective and a deep familiarity with the latest technological trends. By recognizing and valuing these strengths, organizations and individuals can create a more effective and inclusive communication environment.

Incorporating a variety of communication channels is another effective strategy for bridging the generational divide. Offering multiple modes of communication—whether face-to-face meetings, phone calls, emails, or instant messaging—allows everyone to choose the method that works best for them. This flexibility ensures that no one is excluded from the conversation, regardless of their generational preferences. In the workplace, organizations can foster inclusivity by using different communication tools to accommodate a range of styles, ensuring that information flows smoothly across generational lines.

Training programs focused on improving communication across generations can also be beneficial. These programs can teach employees how to communicate effectively with people from different generations, helping them to recognize and appreciate different communication preferences. Workshops can cover topics such as how to use technology in communication, how to give and receive feedback across generations, and how to overcome generational stereotypes. Training helps create a more open and collaborative environment, where individuals from different generations feel comfortable expressing their ideas and working together.

Finally, mentorship programs that encourage cross-generational relationships can be a powerful tool for bridging the communication gap. Mentorship allows older and younger generations to learn from one another, share knowledge, and gain insights into different perspectives. These relationships help to break down stereotypes and foster mutual respect. Younger generations can teach older generations about new technologies, while older generations can offer guidance on professional development and navigating workplace dynamics.

In conclusion, bridging the communication gap between generations is essential for fostering collaboration, reducing misunderstandings, and creating inclusive environments. By promoting active listening, flexibility, empathy, and mutual respect, individuals can overcome the challenges posed by generational differences and communicate effectively with people from all walks of life. Each generation brings unique strengths and perspectives to the table, and by embracing these differences, we can create more productive, harmonious relationships. Whether in the workplace, in education, or in social settings, understanding and bridging generational differences in communication styles is essential for building stronger connections and achieving shared goals.

***Section Closed...***

## *Part-3: Shaping the Culture of Communication: Creating a World Where Words Build, Not Break*

In today's interconnected world, the importance of communication cannot be overstated. Communication is the foundation upon which relationships, businesses, and societies are built. It has the power to unite or divide, uplift or tear down. Words can either create bridges or walls, and the way we communicate shapes our interactions, understanding, and the culture in which we live. The challenge we face today is creating a culture of communication where words build, rather than break.

At its core, effective communication is about more than just sharing information. It is about understanding, connection, and empathy. It is about making sure that the message we intend to convey is received with clarity and respect. In the context of personal, professional, and societal interactions, the ability to communicate with kindness, understanding, and respect has become more important than ever. The global nature of modern communication, driven by technology, means that words can travel faster and reach more people than ever before. This brings both opportunity and responsibility. As we create and share messages, we must be mindful of the impact our words have.

In this chapter, we will explore how the culture of communication is formed, the challenges that arise when communication breaks down, and how we can foster a world where words are used to build, not break. Through understanding the dynamics of communication, the role of empathy, and the power of mindful conversation, we can shape a culture that values positive, respectful, and effective communication.

**The Role of Communication in Society:** Communication is an essential human activity. It is how we connect with others, share our thoughts and feelings, and work toward mutual understanding. From the earliest days of human society, communication has been used to convey ideas, express emotions, and collaborate for the common good. Whether through speech, writing, or non-verbal cues, the way we communicate has always played a key role in shaping our social and cultural environments.

In today's world, communication extends beyond personal interactions. The digital age has created new avenues for communication, including social media platforms, online forums, and instant messaging. While these tools allow for instantaneous communication across the globe, they also bring new challenges. The speed and reach of digital communication can lead to misunderstandings, the spread of misinformation, and even harm. Words, when misused, can have a profound negative impact, damaging relationships, reputations, and even entire communities.

On the flip side, communication has the potential to be a force for good. Words can inspire, motivate, and empower. They can encourage change, promote understanding, and foster collaboration. In every conversation, whether personal or professional, there is an opportunity to choose words that uplift and encourage, rather than words that tear down and divide. By choosing words that are thoughtful, respectful, and constructive, we contribute to building a culture of communication that is positive, inclusive, and effective.

**Understanding the Impact of Words:** Words are powerful tools. They have the ability to shape perceptions, influence behavior, and even create lasting change. The impact of words goes beyond their immediate meaning; it extends to how they are interpreted and the feelings they evoke. For example, a kind word of encouragement can inspire someone to take action or push through challenges. On the other hand, harsh or dismissive words can discourage, hurt, and create feelings of isolation or resentment.

In a professional setting, the language we use can affect everything from team dynamics to company culture. Leaders who communicate with empathy and clarity can motivate their teams, create trust, and foster a positive work environment. Conversely, leaders who use harsh or vague language may create confusion, breed distrust, and hinder productivity. Similarly, in personal relationships, communication is key to building and maintaining trust, respect, and understanding.

One of the challenges in communication today is the increasing reliance on digital platforms. While these platforms offer convenience and reach, they can also reduce the nuance and emotional depth that face-to-face communication offers. The lack of non-verbal cues, such as body language and tone of voice, can lead to misinterpretation and misunderstanding. In addition, the anonymity of online interactions can sometimes lead to a lack of accountability, with people saying things they might not say in person. This disconnect between intent and impact is one of the reasons why communication can sometimes break down, particularly in online environments.

To shape a culture of communication where words build, we must be aware of the power of our words and strive to use them with intention. We must consider how our words may be received, both in terms of their meaning and their emotional impact. Being mindful of this can help us avoid unintentional harm and ensure that our words are used to uplift and inspire.

**The Importance of Empathy in Communication:** Empathy is the ability to understand and share the feelings of another person. It is a key component of effective communication, as it allows us to connect with others on a deeper level. When we communicate with empathy, we are not just sharing information; we are actively seeking to understand the other person's perspective and responding in a way that acknowledges their feelings and experiences.

In a world where communication can easily break down, empathy is more important than ever. It is the foundation of respectful dialogue and conflict resolution. When we listen with empathy, we create space for others to express themselves without fear of judgment. We allow for a more nuanced understanding of issues, which can lead to more productive conversations and better outcomes. Empathy helps to bridge divides, whether those divides are based on culture, generation, or differing opinions.

One of the challenges in fostering empathy in communication is overcoming the tendency to respond based on our own experiences and assumptions. Often, we are quick to judge or offer advice without truly understanding the other person's point of view. This can lead to communication that feels dismissive or invalidating. By practicing active listening and asking open-ended questions, we can create a more empathetic environment where people feel heard and valued.

Empathy is not just about being kind; it is about creating a culture where people feel understood and respected. When we communicate with empathy, we are more likely to build trust and foster positive relationships. In workplaces, schools, and communities, empathy can lead to greater cooperation, improved teamwork, and a sense of belonging.

**Building a Culture of Positive Communication:** To create a world where words build, not break, we must focus on building a culture of positive communication. This involves not only the way we communicate but also the values and principles that guide our communication practices. A culture of positive communication is one in which individuals are encouraged to express themselves openly and honestly, but in a way that is respectful and mindful of others. One of the key aspects of positive communication is creating an environment where feedback is constructive and supportive. Feedback is essential for growth, but it must be delivered in a way that is helpful rather than critical. Instead of focusing on what went wrong, positive communication focuses on solutions and opportunities for improvement. This approach encourages individuals to take responsibility for their actions without feeling attacked or demoralized.

Another important aspect of positive communication is inclusivity. A culture of communication that builds, rather than breaks, must be inclusive of all voices. This means creating spaces where people from different backgrounds, perspectives, and experiences feel safe and valued. It also means actively listening to voices that are often marginalized or silenced, and ensuring that their contributions are heard and respected.

Creating a culture of positive communication also requires leaders to set the tone. Leaders have a responsibility to model the communication behaviors they want to see in their organizations or communities. By demonstrating empathy, respect, and active listening, leaders can foster an environment where these values are reflected in the communication practices of everyone involved. When leaders prioritize positive communication, they create a ripple effect that influences the entire culture.

**Overcoming Challenges in Communication:** While the importance of creating a world where words build is clear, achieving this goal is not without its challenges. One of the biggest challenges is overcoming the natural tendencies we all have toward judgment, defensiveness, and misinterpretation. These tendencies can lead to communication breakdowns and conflict. To overcome these challenges, we must be committed to continuous learning and improvement.

Another challenge is the fast-paced nature of modern communication. With the rise of digital communication, people often expect immediate responses, and this can create pressure to communicate quickly rather than thoughtfully. In these fast-paced environments, it is easy to fall into the trap of reactive communication, where we respond without fully considering the impact of our words. To address this, we must prioritize thoughtful, intentional communication and create spaces where people can engage in more meaningful conversations.

Finally, creating a culture of communication that builds requires a commitment to long-term change. It requires individuals, organizations, and societies to invest in developing their communication skills, practicing empathy, and fostering inclusivity. This is a continuous process that requires patience, reflection, and a willingness to adapt.

Words are powerful, and their impact can extend far beyond the immediate moment. The culture of communication we create today will shape the relationships, institutions, and societies of tomorrow. To build a world where words build, not break, we must commit to mindful, empathetic, and positive communication. By fostering understanding, respect, and inclusivity, we can create a culture where communication is used as a tool for connection, growth, and collaboration.

As we navigate the complexities of communication in our personal and professional lives, let us remember that our words have the power to create, to inspire, and to bring people together. Through intentional and compassionate communication, we can shape a world where words truly build, not break.

***Section Closed…***

### *Part-4: The Misunderstood Link: Introversion and Communication*

In today's fast-paced and digitally connected world, communication is often misunderstood. Many people wrongly believe that communication is limited to being talkative, outspoken, or fluent in English. It is commonly assumed that the more someone speaks, the better communicator they are. However, the real meaning of communication is far deeper than just the ability to speak. True communication is the art of delivering correct and meaningful information in such a way that the other person understands it clearly.

Unfortunately, this deeper understanding is often forgotten. In a world where opinions are shared freely, whether asked for or not, and where misinformation spreads faster than truth, real communication is at risk. People tend to believe the most liked or most shared statement without checking facts. In such a scenario, individuals who choose silence over noise, and depth over drama, are often misunderstood.

**The Rise of Misconceptions:** One of the biggest misconceptions in today's society is around introversion. Introverts, who are naturally quiet, thoughtful, and reserved, are often misunderstood as being weak, socially awkward, or lacking communication skills. Society tends to label introverts as people with mental issues who need counselling or therapy. This judgment is unfair and harmful.

In truth, introversion is a natural personality trait. An introvert is someone who focuses more on their internal world of thoughts and feelings than on the chaos of the external world. They are calm observers who avoid unnecessary drama and are deeply focused on self-growth. They gather useful information, leave out distractions, and think before they act or speak.

Contrary to common belief, being an introvert does not mean being unfriendly, shy, or lacking intelligence. It means choosing silence as a strength. It means having the ability to enjoy life, motivate oneself, and grow without depending on external validation. Introverts are not attention-seekers. They are peace-seekers.

**Common Myths and Realities:** Many false beliefs surround the topic of introversion. Let us take a closer look at how these myths contrast with reality:

| Trait | Misconception | Reality |
| --- | --- | --- |
| Introversion | Poor communicator | Often excellent communicators, especially in writing or deep discussions |
| Quietness | Lack of ideas | Ideas are internalized first, then expressed carefully |
| Group silence | Disengaged | Observing, reflecting, or waiting for the right moment to speak |

These points show how society often misunderstands silence and introverted behavior. Silence is not weakness. It is awareness.

**Being Introvert vs Communication-Misunderstood Relationship:** Communication is usually seen as a social skill, and society often assumes that only extroverts are good at it. Extroverts are known for being energetic, expressive, and quick to respond. Because of this, introverts are mistakenly considered poor communicators. But the relationship between introversion and communication is not that simple. It is more complex and needs thoughtful analysis.

Introverts are not bad at communication. In fact, many introverts are excellent communicators. Their strength lies in the quality and depth of what they say, not in how frequently or loudly they say it. Let us consider a few examples of well-known introverts who have made a huge impact:

- **Bill Gates**, the co-founder of Microsoft, has openly spoken about how being an introvert helped him focus and think deeply. He believes that introverts can succeed by using their unique strengths and working alongside extroverts to create a balanced team.
- **Elon Musk**, known for leading multiple companies, took time and practice to learn how to speak publicly. He once shared that being introverted made it hard at first, but it did not stop him from growing as a leader.
- **Emma Watson**, a well-known actress, has said that she once thought something was wrong with her because she did not enjoy parties. But later she accepted her introverted personality and realized that it was perfectly normal.
- **Eleanor Roosevelt**, a powerful speaker and leader, was actually an introvert. She once said that it is important to have a friendship with yourself first because only then can you be a true friend to others.

These examples show that introverts are not shy or socially incapable. They are just different in how they choose to express themselves.

**Introverts Communicate Differently:** Introverts do not avoid communication. They simply prefer environments where they can express themselves comfortably. They seek meaningful conversations instead of small talk. They prefer to write rather than speak in crowded rooms. For them, communication is about connection, not performance.

**Thoughtful Speakers:** Introverts think before they speak. This means their words are more likely to be meaningful, clear, and respectful. While extroverts might talk to think, introverts think to talk. They process their thoughts quietly and speak when they have something valuable to say.

**Active Listeners:** Introverts are excellent listeners. They don't interrupt. They don't dominate conversations. They listen to understand, not just to respond. This makes them wonderful teammates, friends, and partners. Their ability to pay attention to details makes their conversations insightful.

**Depth Over Breadth:** Introverts prefer deep conversations. They like to discuss ideas, emotions, and meaningful topics rather than gossip or surface-level subjects. They are not fans of large gatherings but thrive in one-on-one or small group interactions.

**Writing as a Strength:** Many introverts shine in written communication. Writing allows them to take time to express their ideas thoughtfully. Emails, messages, articles, or reports give them space to be creative and clear. They may struggle in spontaneous speaking situations, but when given time to prepare, they often outperform their extroverted peers.

**Workplace Challenges and Realities:** The workplace is one of the main places where introverts are often misunderstood. Meetings are usually fast-paced and dominated by those who speak first and loudest. In such spaces, introverts can appear quiet or inactive. But in truth, they are observing, analyzing, and preparing to contribute meaningfully. Organizations need to recognize different communication styles. Leaders should understand that not everyone is comfortable speaking on the spot. Giving agendas in advance, allowing written feedback, and creating smaller group discussions can help introverts feel more included. Introverted leaders often lead with calmness, thoughtfulness, and strong listening skills. They may not be the most energetic in the room, but they build trust and loyalty through their focused and intentional leadership style.

**Strengths Hidden in Silence:** Introverts have many hidden strengths. Let us explore some of them:

- **Written Communication**: They express ideas more clearly when writing.
- **Empathetic Listening**: They listen with care and understanding.
- **Conflict Resolution**: They handle conflicts calmly without adding to drama.
- **Deep Conversations**: They connect through thoughtful & honest discussions.

These strengths are highly valuable in both personal and professional settings. They are not just soft skills but are essential tools for building lasting relationships.

**Redefining What a Good Communicator Is:** It is time to rethink what it means to be a good communicator. It is not about being the loudest or the most visible. It is about making others feel heard and understood. It is about clarity, connection, and trust.

Many introverts excel at communication because they understand the value of words. They don't speak to impress. They speak to express. Their words may be fewer, but their meaning is stronger.

**Supporting Introverted Communicators:** If you are an introvert or working with one, here are some ways to support and encourage better communication:

- **Do not confuse silence with weakness**: Give them time to think before expecting a reply.
- **Let them prepare**: Share meeting topics or discussion points in advance.
- **Use written methods**: Encourage emails, reports, or chats as ways of expressing thoughts.
- **Accept their style**: Do not force them to change. Let them communicate in ways that are natural to them.

By doing these simple things, we create an environment where everyone, including introverts, feels valued and heard.

**The Bigger Picture:** The relationship between introversion and communication is not a battle between silence and speech. It is a balance between thinking and speaking, listening and expressing, observing and engaging. Both introverts and extroverts bring value to the conversation in different ways. The modern world needs to welcome all communication styles. Schools, colleges, and workplaces must be educated about the power of thoughtful engagement. Society should stop treating silence as a problem. Instead, it should see it as a sign of intelligence, self-awareness, and focus. We must remember that not all strength is loud. Some strength is quiet, steady, and deeply rooted. It is time to recognize, respect, and celebrate this quiet strength.

Introversion is not incompetence. It is not a flaw or a weakness. It is a way of being, a way of thinking, and a way of communicating. When society labels introverts as less capable just because they are less talkative, it creates a false and harmful narrative.

Through this book, and through the message of "Verbatique," we aim to break these false labels. We want every introvert to feel seen, heard, and understood. We want society to accept that communication is not only about volume, but also about value. Let us open the door to deeper connections, meaningful conversations, and a world where every voice matters; even the quiet ones.

***Section Closed...***

## CONCLUSION: THE POWER OF COMMUNICATION IN SHAPING OUR WORLD

As we wrap up this extensive conversation, it's clear that communication is the cornerstone of everything we do, whether in our personal lives, at work, or in broader society. The themes we explored, from the complexities of understanding others' perspectives to mastering the art of listening and speaking with clarity, are all integral parts of fostering meaningful connections and interactions.

We began by recognizing the importance of communication in a professional setting and how it influences everything from interviews and workplace interactions to leadership. We saw that clear, effective communication requires a blend of verbal and non-verbal skills, active listening, and the ability to adapt to various contexts and audiences. These skills, when honed, not only elevate personal interactions but also contribute to a collaborative and productive environment.

One of the key takeaways was the understanding that communication is not one-size-fits-all. It is shaped by culture, generational influences, and individual experiences. As we explored topics like bridging generational communication gaps and navigating cross-cultural environments, it became evident that the ability to adapt and be mindful of these differences is crucial in creating inclusive, harmonious spaces.

Moreover, we delved into the psychological aspects of communication, recognizing that empathy, emotional intelligence, and the ability to manage misunderstandings or conflicts play a pivotal role in fostering positive relationships. In a world that can sometimes feel fragmented, communication remains a powerful tool for connection, problem-solving, and growth.

Ultimately, what we have learned from this discussion is that communication is far more than just exchanging information; it is about creating understanding, building trust, and forging connections that transcend barriers. It is about cultivating a culture where words build, not break. Every conversation we engage in offers an opportunity to shape our relationships, our communities, and our world for the better.

In conclusion, the journey towards becoming a better communicator is ongoing. Whether we are speaking, listening, or leading, we must remain conscious of the impact our words and actions have on those around us. Through continuous learning and application of the principles we've discussed, we have the power to influence not only our personal growth but also the world in which we live. As you move forward, remember that communication is a skill that can always be refined. Each interaction is an opportunity to practice, to listen more intently, and to speak with intention.

*** BE A GOOD COMMUNICATOR ***

***Communication is the thread that connects the past, present, and future. As we grow, so must the way we connect.***

www.ingramcontent.com/pod-product-compliance
Lightning Source LLC
Chambersburg PA
CBHW041732100726
47973CB00011B/185
*9798899066702*